I0160082

Book Two

Understanding Spoken English

a focus on everyday language in context

Susan Boyer

Revised cover edition, 2014

Boyer Educational Resources 2003
reprinted 2004, 2005, 2006, 2007, 2012

Published by
Boyer Educational Resources
for worldwide distribution.

Phone/fax +61 2 4739 1538
E-mail: boyer@eftel.net.au
Web address: www.boyereducation.com.au

Acknowledgments

I would like to express my thanks to the following people for their contribution to the final presentation of this book:

Firstly, I would like to thank all the teachers who trialed exercises and material contained in the original (Australian) edition of this book and suggested improvements. In particular I wish to say thank you to Terry Stroble for his time and constructive comments regarding North American usage of expressions included in this book.

I would like to thank Matthew Larwood for his creative illustrations. I would like to say thank you to Darrell Hilton Productions for the production of the accompanying audio recordings. And, as with all my previous English language teaching publications, I am particularly indebted to the many students who have given me the necessary insight into the language needs of English language learners around the world.

Again, I want to thank my dear husband, Len, for his encouragement and support throughout the project, as well as the many hours spent in the production of this resource.

Illustrations on pages 18, 28, 38, 41, 42, 54, 63b, 64, 72, 86, 96, 107 are by Matthew J Larwood.

Other images used herein were obtained from IMSI's MasterClips Collection, 1895 Francisco Blvd. East, San Rafael, CA 94901-5506, USA. Also, Greenstreet software Ltd, Meadow Lane, St Ives, Cambridgeshire PE27 4LG UK
The kookaburra clipart was obtained from Australian Graphics Selection, New Horizons, Armidale. Australia.

Boyer, Susan
Understanding Spoken English: a focus on everyday language in context – Book Two
ISBN 1 877074 12 8

1. English language - Spoken English - Textbooks for foreign speakers.
2. English language - Spoken English - Problems, exercises, etc. I. Boyer Educational Resources
II Title

428.34

Boyer Educational Resources
PO Box 255, Glenbrook, 2773 Australia,
Phone/Fax +61 2 4739 1538

Dear English Language Student,

Welcome to **Book Two** in the *'Understanding Spoken English – a focus on everyday language in context'* series. This book, along with its accompanying audio recording, has been designed to help you to understand English as it is spoken in 'everyday' situations in English speaking environments around the world. As a student of English as a second or foreign language, you are no doubt aware of the difference between the formally presented language of many textbooks and the speech you hear, outside the language classroom, in the English speaking media or in conversations with native English speakers.

As well as introducing and explaining the meaning of many widely used everyday expressions, each unit focuses on other aspects of spoken English, such as grammatical forms used when talking about the past and the future and the use of articles (*a, an, the*). Aspects of pronunciation, such as pronouncing 'ed' endings on words and the use of intonation to show meaning, is dealt within the context of everyday conversations. You will also learn conversational strategies involved in everyday situations such as making a telephone call, giving advice, giving instructions and directions and giving feedback.

I sincerely hope you enjoy and benefit from using *Understanding Spoken English - a focus on everyday language in context - Book Two*

Susan Boyer

A note on 'English' accents used in the audio recording

The conversations on the accompanying audio recording present speakers with a variety of different English accents as they are encountered in English speaking environments around the world. This is because it is very beneficial for students to become accustomed to the different accents of English speakers that will be encountered in the media, in international business contexts and social situations.

The intention of presenting different accents, however, is not to provide particular models for imitation but to *increase familiarity* with a variety of different accents.

It should be noted that, though the *accents* of the speakers vary, the vocabulary and grammar points presented in each unit of this book are those generally used by <u>all</u> varieties of 'native speaker' English.

ABOUT THIS BOOK

Understanding Spoken English- Book Two has been designed so that you can work through it alone, without the help of a teacher, or in a classroom situation with other students. The book contains nine units of work, each based on a conversation about a particular topic. The units are divided into **six parts** that have been designed to introduce unfamiliar language, **step by step,** in a gradual and systematic way. The layout of the book is as follows:

Part 1 - Focus on listening for general understanding

Part 1 introduces the topic and invites you to listen to an everyday conversation and answer a few general questions by putting a tick next to the correct answers. You will be listening for **general** understanding of the conversation only. (You will not need to understand every word.) This is an important step as it will help you to realise that it's not always necessary to hear every word to understand the general meaning of a conversation. In some units, you are asked to check words in a dictionary, so have a dictionary nearby when you are studying.

Part 2 - Focus on reading & finding the meaning

In this section, you will **read** Conversation 1 as you listen again. When you have finished listening, your task is to **compare Conversation 1 with Conversation 2** (which will be next to Conversation 1). Conversation 1 contains the everyday expressions and Conversation 2 contains an interpretation of the expressions in Conversation 1. This section will help you to learn the **meaning** of the everyday expressions.

Part 3 - Focus on listening for detail

Now you will listen to Conversation 1 again and write in the missing words in the spaces as you hear them. Don't worry about spelling as this exercise focuses on your **listening skills** - you can check your spelling later. Listen to the conversation as many times as you like, then check your answers (and spelling) by comparing what you have written with Conversation 1.

Part 4 - Focus on listening and writing for reinforcement

This section reinforces (strengthens) your memory as you listen once more to Conversation 1 and tick the newly learnt everyday expressions on the list as you hear them. Then you are asked to look at the list of expressions (all taken from Conversation 1) and try to remember their meaning. Write in the ones that you can remember, then check your answers by reading Conversation 1 again or checking the reference list at the back of the book. This may seem like hard work but **writing** the meanings of the newly learnt expressions is a useful way of reinforcing what you have just heard and read.

Part 5 - Focus on language revision - crosswords

Now it's time to test yourself and see what you have learnt by trying the language revision and crossword activity. In this section, you are asked to use the newly learned expressions in a different context. In each unit you are asked to complete sentences with the appropriate expression and complete the crossword. The answers to the exercises can be found in the answer section of this book.

Part 6 - Focus on other aspects of spoken English

In this section, there will be exercises for you to complete and/or cultural advice for you to remember. This section focuses on aspects of spoken English (grammar, pronunciation etc.) that may make it difficult for learners to understand. Each unit focuses on conversation strategies or social conventions used by the speakers in Conversation 1 of that particular unit.

Language Reviews

After Unit 3, Unit 6 and Unit 9 you will find a language review that consists of pictures and sentences containing the 'everyday' expressions, which were introduced in the preceding units, for you to match together. This will help you to see how much you have remembered.

IMPORTANT NOTE TO STUDENTS

Please be aware that the meaning of colloquial language is *very dependent on the context or situation in which it is used.* 'Understanding Spoken English' has been designed to *introduce and explain* the meaning of colloquial expressions used by English speakers in the everyday situations presented in this book. However, because colloquial expressions can have different meanings in different situations, it is not recommended that students of English immediately begin using the newly introduced expressions indiscriminately. It would be much better to spend time becoming familiar with, and understanding the correct meaning of expressions in different situations *before you use them* in your conversations.

In this regard, the author and publisher of this book will not be responsible to any person, with regard to the misuse of language, caused directly or indirectly by the information presented in this book.

UNDERSTANDING SPOKEN ENGLISH – BOOK TWO

CONTENTS

UNDERSTANDING SPOKEN ENGLISH – BOOK TWO

CONTENTS

GLOSSARY OF LANGUAGE TERMS

Use this list as a reference while you are using this book.

adjective: a word which describes things (**black** car), people (**beautiful** girl), places (**multicultural** city) or events (**exciting** race), etc. See Unit 4, Part 6B.

alphabet: The English alphabet consists of twenty six letters:
a, b, c, d, e, f, g, h, i, j, k, l, m, n, o, p, q, r, s, t, u, v, w, x, y, z.

These letters are categorised into **vowels**: a, e, i, o, u.
and **consonants**: b, c, d, f, g, h, j, k, l, m, n, p, q, r, s, t, v, w, x, y, z.
(The consonant letter 'y' can be pronounced as a vowel sound; for example: 'g<u>y</u>m'.)

article: The words *'a', 'an', 'the'* are called articles. See Unit 3, Part 6A for details on use.

auxiliary verb: a 'helper' verb which can be used with another verb to form tense. (eg. <u>**will**</u> come, <u>**did**</u> come, <u>**have**</u> come) Modal auxiliary verbs are used with another verb to show mood or manner. (eg. <u>**should**</u> come, <u>**might**</u> come, <u>**must**</u> come).

discourse marker: Discourse markers **show connection** between what has already been said and what will come next in a stretch of discourse.. (eg.'*...however,..*', '*and I'm sure you'll agree...*'). A discourse marker is also a word or expression which shows the speaker's attitude to what is being said. eg. '*In fact,.....*', '*...and of course...*'

ellipsis: the omission of words from a sentence when the meaning is clear without them, due to the context of the conversation. eg. *Anything else? (meaning '<u>Is there any thing else?</u>* '

imperative: base (simple) form of a verb, used at the beginning of a sentence, to give orders, instructions, directions. (eg. <u>**Be**</u> quiet; <u>**Turn**</u> right there). See Unit 7, Part 6A.

infinitive: the base form of a verb, usually with 'to' eg. It's easy <u>**to do**</u>. I want <u>**to start**</u> now.

intonation: Intonation refers to the way our voice goes up and down in pitch when speaking.

noun: a word which names **things,** (eg. car, sky); **places** (eg. New Zealand, ocean) **people** (eg. John, President), as well as **abstract things** - things we can't see but can experience/talk about. (eg. history, pain, ideas, education).

phrasal verb: A verb that consists of two parts: a base verb and an adverbial particle. eg. 'pick up', 'try on'

phonemic symbols: See the explanation below for 'sound symbols'.

pronoun: a word which is used in place of a noun. eg. *it, she, they.* (See Part 6 of Units 5 & 6)

schwa: The symbol 'ə', and the sound it represents, are referred to as 'schwa'. The symbol 'ə' (schwa) is used in most dictionaries to represent weak, unstressed syllables in words.

sound symbols: also called **phonemic symbols** – these symbols represent the sounds of English. English sounds are generally divided into two main categories: **vowel** sounds, and **consonant** sounds. The vowel sounds can be further divided into simple vowel sounds and **diphthong** sounds. Diphthongs can be defined as 'two vowel sounds linked or glided together within a syllable'. For example, the vowel sound in the word 'v<u>oi</u>ce' consists of two linked vowels sounds and is represented by the symbol /ɔɪ/.

See the Phonemic Chart of English Sounds on page 129 that shows the sound symbols of English, along with example words to demonstrate each sound.

GLOSSARY OF LANGUAGE TERMS

stress: In spoken language, **stress** refers to the emphasis of a word or syllable within a word.

word stress: In words with more than one syllable, one sound is usually stronger (spoken more clearly) than the other(s). The term, **stressed syllable**, refers to the strongest (primary) sound in words of more than one syllable.

sentence stress: Words which carry the main message of the sentence contain *stressed* syllables. Stressing the important words helps the listener to hear the message of the speaker. eg. I *want* to go *home*.

syllable: Spoken words are formed with **syllables**, meaning **units of sound.** A syllable is a unit of unbroken sound, generally containing a vowel sound.

verb: a word which shows **action**. eg. He *ran* all the way.
or **state/experience**. eg. She *is* a student. I *feel* cold.

‘Base form’ can refer to the simple present form of the verb. eg. **be, go, see.**

verb tenses: Tenses show the **time** of an action, event or condition. Some examples are:

past simple tense: indicates finished past action. eg. He *went* to Asia last year.

present perfect tense: a) used for an action/experience which began in the past and has continued to the present. eg. I *have lived* here since 1998. eg. 1998

b) used when a past action/experience (which happened at an unspecified time) has present significance.
eg.. He *has been* to Asia.

present simple tense: a) indicates a present condition/fact.
eg. I *am* hungry. eg.

b) indicates a present routine. eg. I *work* four days each week. eg.

present progressive: (also called present continuous) a verb form made with *am/are/is +…ing*.
a) This tense is used to talk about an action which is happening at the time of speaking. eg. We *are waiting* for him.

b) The present progressive is also used to refer to a future arrangement.
eg. He *is leaving* tomorrow.

future simple tense: will +verb indicates future time. eg. I think, it *will rain* tomorrow.

vowel sounds: See notes under 'sound symbols' on the previous page.

NOTE:
This list is not intended as a complete guide. Refer to a comprehensive grammar book for more details.

UNIT 1

A TELEPHONE ENQUIRY

I hope I haven't missed the boat again.

There's a lot of red tape involved and it's still up in the air so I wouldn't count on it...

Listening for general understanding

Listen to this conversation in which Chris is phoning a college for information about a course he is interested in. (Unit 1 on the audio recording.) The conversation contains everyday expressions that will be explained later in the unit - so don't worry if you don't understand every word. This time you are only listening for a general understanding of the topic. As you listen, tick the correct answers below.

When you have finished you can check your answers on page 108.

1) Chris is inquiring about:

    a) an Aviation Course.

    b) an Office Skills Course.

    c) an English Language Course.

2) When did the course start?

    a) last week

    b) three days ago

    c) three weeks ago

3) Chris can't join the class because:

    a) it's too late to start.

    b) the class is full.

    c) the class was cancelled.

4) On which date does the computing course start:

    a) 5th

    b) 15th

    c) 16th

5) The spelling of Chris's surname is:

    a) Eslee

    b) Lea

    c) Lee

Now, we'll look at the everyday expressions used in the conversation – turn to the next page.

CONVERSATION 1 (with everyday expressions)

◀◀ Replay Conversation 1
Read this conversation as you listen to the audio recording. Do you know what the _underlined_ words mean? They are colloquial or 'everyday' expressions.

Receptionist:	West Town Institute. Can I help you?
Chris:	Yes. Is that the business college?
Receptionist:	That's right.
Chris:	I'd like to speak to someone about joining the Office Skills Course please.
Receptionist:	**Hold the line** please. I'll **put you through**.
Assistant:	Office Administration. Can I help you?
Chris:	Yes. I'd like to join the Office Skills Course for this term, please.
Assistant:	I'm sorry, that course is already **under way** for this term. It started three weeks ago. But I can **put you down** for the next course if you like.
Chris:	I'd really like to start now, if I can. Would it still be possible to join this class?
Assistant:	I'll just check for you but as **a rule of thumb** the **cut off** date for joining a class is two weeks after the start of the course. I'll just check … I'm sorry, the course you're interested in is completely full and unfortunately our next course is full as well. I can **take your details** and let you know if any places become available for next term. There's **the off chance** that someone may **pull out**.
Chris:	Yes OK, thank you. Will there be only one Office Skills class next term?
Assistant:	Well, there's a possibility of a second class but there's a lot of **red tape** involved and it's still **up in the air** so **I wouldn't count on it**... Actually, I've just noticed on the computer that there's been a cancellation in one of our computing courses that begin next week. That may be useful for you.
Chris:	Oh, yes that'd be good. When does it start and how much is it?
Assistant:	It starts on the 15th. The cost depends on which subjects you do. I can send some information with an application form if you like but you'll have to let us know **ASAP**. Places usually get **snapped up** as soon as they become available and I'm sure you don't want to **miss the boat** again.
Chris:	That's for sure.
Assistant:	OK. Could I have your name and address please?
Chris:	Yes, it's Mr. Chris Lea.
Assistant:	Sorry, I didn't **catch** that. Did you say Eslee?
Chris:	No. My first name's Chris. My surname is Lea. That's L, E, A. My address is….

Now let's see what the underlined expressions mean - look at the next page.

CONVERSATION 2 (explanation of everyday expressions)

Compare Conversation 1 with Conversation 2 - You will see that some of the words are different but the meaning is the same in both conversations. Find the underlined words in Conversation 1, then underline the words with the same meaning in Conversation 2. For example: *Hold the line*. (Conversation 1) = *Wait a moment*. (Conversation 2)

Receptionist:	West Town Institute. Can I help you?
Chris:	Yes. Is that the business college?
Receptionist:	That's right.
Chris:	I'd like to speak to someone about joining the Office Skills Course please.
Receptionist:	Wait a moment, please. I'll connect you to the department.
Assistant:	Office Administration. Can I help you?
Chris:	Yes. I'd like to join the Office Skills course for this term, please.
Assistant:	I'm sorry, that course is already in progress for this term. It started three weeks ago. But I can write your name on the list for the next course if you like.
Chris:	I'd really like to start now, if I can. Would it still be possible to join this class?
Assistant:	I'll just check for you but as a general rule the last possible date for joining a class is two weeks after the start of the course. I'll just check…I'm sorry, the course you're interested in is completely full and unfortunately our next course is full as well. I can record your name and address and let you know if any places become available for next term. There's the very small chance that someone may cancel or withdraw.
Chris:	Yes OK, thank you. Will there be only one Office Skills class next term?
Assistant:	Well, there's a possibility of a second class but there's a lot of official rules involved and it's still undecided so don't expect it to happen... Actually, I've just noticed on the computer that there's been a cancellation in one of our computing courses that begin next week. That may be useful for you.
Chris:	Oh, yes that'd be good. When does it start and how much is it?
Assistant:	It starts on the 15th. The cost depends on which subjects you do. I can send some information with an application form if you like but you'll have to let us know as soon as possible. Places usually get taken/accepted quickly as soon as they become available and I'm sure you don't want to lose/miss the opportunity again.
Chris:	That's for sure.
Assistant:	OK. Could I have your name and address please?
Chris:	Yes, it's Mr. Chris Lea.
Assistant:	Sorry, I didn't hear/understand that. Did you say Eslee?
Chris:	No. My first name's Chris. My surname is Lea. That's L, E, A. My address is….

Important note:
The language used in Conversation 2 (above) may seem easier to understand when compared with Conversation 1. However, the 'everyday' expressions used in Conversation 1 are used extensively by speakers of English. Therefore it is beneficial to become familiar with the everyday expressions used by the speakers in **Conversation 1**.

◀◀ Replay Conversation 1

Listen to the conversation again and fill in the missing words. You may have to listen more than once. (Don't worry about your spelling as this exercise focuses on listening skills - you can check your spelling later.)

Receptionist:	West Town Institute. Can I help you?
Chris:	Yes. Is that the business college?
Receptionist:	That's right.
Chris:	I'd like to speak to someone about joining the Office Skills Course please.
Receptionist:	**Hold the** _____ please. I'll _____ **you through**.
Assistant:	Office Administration. Can I help you?
Chris:	Yes. I'd like to join the Office Skills Course for this term, please.
Assistant:	I'm sorry, that course is already _____ **way** for this term. It started three weeks ago. But I can **put you** _____ for the next course if you like.
Chris:	I'd really like to start now, if I can. Would it still be possible to join this class?
Assistant:	I'll just check for you but as **a rule of** _____ the **cut** _____ date for joining a class is two weeks after the start of the course. I'll just check… I'm sorry, the course you're interested in is completely full and unfortunately our next course is full as well. I can _____ **your details** and let you know if any places become available for next term. There's **the** _____ **chance** that someone may **pull** _____.
Chris:	Yes OK, thank you. Will there be only one Office Skills class next term?
Assistant:	Well, there's a possibility of a second class but there's a lot of _____ **tape** involved and it's still **up in the** _____ so **I wouldn't** _____ **on it**… Actually, I've just noticed on the computer that there's been a cancellation in one of our computing courses that begin next week. That may be useful for you.
Chris:	Oh, yes that'd be good. When does it start and how much is it?
Assistant:	It starts on the 15th. The cost depends on which subjects you do. I can send you some information with an application form if you like, but you'll have to let us know **ASAP**. Places usually get **snapped** _____ as soon as they become available and I'm sure you don't want to **miss the** _____ again.
Chris:	That's for sure.
Assistant:	OK. Could I have your name and address please?
Chris:	Yes, it's Mr. Chris Lea.
Assistant:	Sorry, I didn't _____ that. Did you say Eslee?
Chris:	No. My first name's Chris. My surname is Lea. That's L, E, A. My address is….

> Now check your answers by comparing this page with CONVERSATION 1.

In order to become more familiar with these new everyday expressions:

◀◀ Replay Conversation 1
1) Listen and tick the boxes ☑ next to the expressions as you hear them.
2) Write the definitions you can remember. (The first one has been done as an example.)
   Check your answers with the reference list on page 119.

☐ hold the line............................. *Wait a moment* _____

☐ put (you) through......................... _____

☐ under way................................ _____

☐ put (you) down .... _____

☐ a rule of thumb........................... _____

☐ cut off (date)............................. _____

☐ take (your) details....................... _____

☐ the off chance........................... _____

☐ pull out.................................. _____

☐ red tape................................. _____

☐ up in the air............................. _____

☐ I wouldn't count on it................... _____

☐ ASAP.................................... _____

☐ snapped up.............................. _____

☐ miss the boat........................... _____

☐ catch.................................... _____

LANGUAGE NOTES:

• 'I wouldn't *count on* it', can also be expressed as 'I wouldn't *bank on* it'
  or... 'Don't *count on* it', can also be expressed as...... 'Don't *bank on* it'.

• *ASAP* (as soon as possible) can also be written as *a.s.a.p*.

CROSSWORD - LANGUAGE REVISION

Complete the sentences, choosing from the everyday expressions that are listed below.
You can use the clues in brackets ( ) at the end of each sentence to help you.
Then complete the crossword using the everyday expressions you have written.
The first one has been done as an example. The answers are on page 108.

rule of thumb	off chance	up in the air	snapped up	put me down	~~red tape~~
under way	miss the boat	hold the line	your details	count on	catch

ACROSS

1) There's a lot of _**red tape**_ involved when trying to make changes in government. (official rules)
3) I'm sorry I didn't _____ your name. (hear/understand)
5) As a _____ ___ _____ you should eat some fruit and vegetables everyday. (general rule)
7) The manager is taking another call. Could you _____ ____ _____ please. (wait a moment)
9) The meeting had been _____ _____ for more than an hour when he arrived. (in progress)
11) I'll have to hurry and get this job application in by the closing date or I'll _____ ____ _____. (lose an opportunity)

DOWN

2) You can ____ ___ _____ to work on Saturday and Sunday if you like, as I need the extra money. (write my name on the list)
4) All the tickets for the concert were _____ ___ weeks ago. There aren't any left. (taken quickly)
6) Write _____ _____ on the form and put it in the box, if you want a chance to win a car. (your name and address etc)
8) I phoned on the ___ _____ that he may be home, but he was out as usual.(very small chance)
10) Susan said she would be early but don't _____ ____ it. She is usually late. (expect/rely on)
12) My travel plans are ____ ___ _____ _____ as my car needs a lot of repairs and I can't afford to repair it. (uncertain/undecided)

FOCUS ON SPOKEN LANGUAGE

Telephoning Strategies

A) Checking information such as correct place/number

◀◀ **Replay Conversation 1**
Listen to the first part of Conversation 1 again and notice how quickly the receptionist says the company name. It is often difficult to hear a company name clearly on the telephone when it is spoken quickly, especially if English is not your first language.

Notice that Chris overcame the problem by checking that he had contacted the right place. Listen to Conversation 1 again. What question did he ask? Write the caller's question below.

Chris:_____ Answer, page 108.

B) Giving a reason for the phone call

When making an enquiry by phone, it's important to clearly state the reason for your call. Notice how Chris introduced his call in Conversation 1.

To the Receptionist:
'I'd like to speak to someone about joining the Office Skills course, please.'

To the Assistant:
'I'd like to join the Office Skills course for this term, please.'

Notice the pattern - I'd like to + verb
↓

To the receptionist:	'I'd like to	*speak* to someone about joining the Office Skills course, please.'
To the assistant:	'I'd like to	*join* the Office Skills course for this term, please.'

Practice

Using the information in sections A) and B) above, complete the following telephone conversation Imagine you are phoning a college to enquire about an English course that was advertised in the newspaper.

Receptionist: West Town College. Can I help you?
You: Yes. _____?
Receptionist: Yes. That's right.
You: I'd like to _____

_____please.

Receptionist: Hold the line please. I'll put you through.
Assistant: Good afternoon, English department. Can I help you?
You: Yes. I'd like to _____

_____, please.

Revision - Aspects of Pronunciation

In *Understanding Spoken English - Book One*, aspects of pronunciation in connected speech, such as the use of 'weak forms' and 'linking' between words were examined.
The following section of this unit revises these aspects of spoken English.

C) Noticing 'weak forms' in spoken English

In spoken English, speakers *stress* the words that are considered most *important* to their message. These words are given more emphasis than other words in the message. They are spoken more clearly than the other words.

For example, in the following sentence,
the words in **bold** type are stressed.
They are the most important words to the message.

'The **books** are on the **desk**.'

Words that do *not* carry the main message
of the speaker are spoken quickly and softly;
they are weak or unstressed.

Some very common words in English, such as *'the', 'a', 'for', 'at', 'to', 'an', 'and', 'of'*
are often pronounced with a weak pronunciation as they do not (usually) provide the important information in the message. When these words are pronounced with a weak sound, they are referred to as *weak forms* (meaning *unstressed words)*. The pronunciation of the weak, unstressed sound of English is generally represented in dictionaries as the symbol ə.

Practice
Read the following section from the beginning Conversation 1 and decide which words are missing.

Chris: I'd like ___ speak ___ someone about joining the Office Skills course please.
Receptionist: Hold ____ line, please. I'll put you through.

◀◀ Replay Conversation 1
Listen to the first few lines of Conversation 1 and check your answers. As you listen, notice the weak pronunciation of the words you have written. You can also check your answers on page 108.

Note: When the word '***the***' comes before a word with an initial vowel sound, as in 'th**e o**ffice' or 'th**e o**ff chance, '***the***' is generally pronounced with a long vowel sound (as in the word th**ese**) and **not** pronounced as a weak form.

D) Word linking in spoken English

When spoken at natural conversational speed, English words are not always heard distinctly, but are often linked together. Some examples are given below.

* **Linking of consonant sounds between words**

Linking occurs between words when **the final consonant sound** of a word is the **same as the first sound of the following word**. eg. the **'s'** sounds in bu**s** **s**top are linked into one sound.

◀◀ **Replay Conversation 1**

Listen to the receptionist's pronunciation of 'West Town' in the first line of Conversation 1. You will hear that Wes**t** **T**own is linked together to become Wes(t) **T**own. (The consonant sound is said only once.)

Try *linking* these words together by pronouncing the final and initial consonants only *once*.

ba**d d**ay	nex**t t**erm
to**p p**lace	joi**n n**ow
bu**s s**top	offic**(e) s**kills (note that 'e' is silent in 'office')

- **Linking of final consonants and initial vowel sounds**

In spoken English, speakers also tend to link the *final consonant sound* of one word to the *initial vowel sound* of the following word. Look at the following sentences, which have been taken from the introduction of Conversation 1.

Tow**n I**nstitute becomes Tow**n i**nstitute   Ca**n I** help becomes Ca**n I** help

◀◀ **Replay Conversation 1**

Listen to the first line of Conversation 1 on the audio recording.
Can you hear the way the words are linked?

> Receptionist: West Tow**n I**nstitute. Ca**n I** help you?

Now pronounce these expressions from Conversation 1, by linking the final consonant of the first word with the initial vowel of the next word.

pull out	becomes	pul**l o**ut	**cut off** date	becomes	cu**t o**ff date
up in the air	becomes	u**p i**n the air	**snapped up**	becomes	snappe**d u**p

> **Remember!** Linking generally occurs between words when:
>
> - the final consonant sound of one word is the same as the first sound
>   of the following word. eg. bu**s s**top becomes bu**ss**top
>
> - the final consonant sound of one word joins with the initial vowel sound
>   of the following word. eg. loo**k o**ut becomes loo**k o**ut

Note:
It is not absolutely necessary for learners of English to link words in their own speech to *be understood* by others. It is important however, for students to be *aware* of these features of spoken language in order *to understand* the connected speech of native English speakers and to realise that the use of these features helps the smooth flow of speech.

UNIT 2

TALKING ABOUT STUDY PROBLEMS

Many students don't ask for help with study problems until it's almost too late to improve their situation. This may be because of embarrassment, laziness or because they don't know that help is available. Have you (or someone you know) ever been in this situation?

Listening for general understanding

Listen to this conversation between friends who are talking about a problem at school. (Unit 2 on the audio recording.) The conversation contains everyday expressions that will be explained later in the unit - so don't worry if you don't understand every word. This time you are only listening for a general understanding of the topic. As you listen, tick the correct answers below. (There may be more than one correct answer.)

1) Lynn is worried because:

        a) her teacher is sick.

        b) she is sick.

        c) her teacher is not pleased with her. assignment.

        d) she may fail her course.

2) She is planning to:

        a) go to the doctor.

        b) leave college.

        c) go overseas to study.

3) Her friend suggests that she should:

        a) transfer to a different course.

        b) go on a holiday.

        c) ask the teacher how she can improve her assignment.

You can check your answers on page 109.

Now, we'll look at the everyday expressions used in the conversation – turn to the next page.

CONVERSATION 1 (with everyday expressions)

◀◀ Replay Conversation 1
Read this conversation as you listen to the audio recording. Do you know what the _underlined_ words mean? They are colloquial or 'everyday' expressions.

Adam: How're you going?

Lynn: Oh, not very well really.

Adam: Why? **What's up**?

Lynn: Oh, it's this course I'm doing. I'm just **not keeping up**.

Adam: Well…

Lynn: I know, it's my fault. In the beginning I was **too laid-back**; thinking it'd be **a piece of cake**. I didn't even **turn up to** most classes. Well, I've just received my major assignment back and the teacher said it's **not up to par** …and the way things are looking I'll probably fail.

Adam: So what're you going to do now?

Lynn: I've been thinking about it and I've decided to **drop out**. It seems I'm **not cut out for** this course.

Adam: You can't be serious. You can't **throw in the towel** now. Think of all the time you've **put in**.

Lynn: I know, I've thought of that but I don't think I have much choice.

Adam: Oh, **come on**! There're other options to just **giving up**.

Lynn: Like what?

Adam: Well, maybe you could transfer to a course more suited to you.

Lynn: No. I **don't stand a chance** of getting into another course now – it's too late. Besides, I'd prefer to **see this course through** if I'm going to do anything.

Adam: Well in that case, why don't you go and talk to your teacher. Say that you're going to **knuckle down** from now on and ask for **some pointers** on how you can improve your assignment.

Lynn: Mm. I could do that. If I really **get stuck into it**, I'm sure I could **catch up** on the work I've missed. I would like to **get through** this course. OK I'll **give it a go**.

Adam: **That's more like it**!

If I really get stuck into it, I'm sure I can catch up.

Now let's see what these expressions mean - look at the next page.

CONVERSATION 2 (explanation of everyday expressions)

Compare Conversation 1 with Conversation 2 -You will see that some of the words are different but the meaning is the same in both conversations. Find the underlined words in Conversation 1, then underline the words with the same meaning in Conversation 2. For example: *What's up?* (Conversation 1) = *What's the problem?* (Conversation 2)

Adam: How're you going?

Lynn: Oh, not very well really.

Adam: Why? <u>What's the problem</u>?

Lynn: Oh, it's this course I'm doing. I'm just not progressing (at the expected rate).

Adam: Well….

Lynn: I know, it's my fault. In the beginning I was too relaxed/lazy; thinking it'd be an easy task. I didn't even attend/arrive at most classes. Well, I've just received my major assignment back and the teacher said it's not of an acceptable level/standard…and the way things are looking I'll probably fail.

Adam: So what're you going to do now?

Lynn: I've been thinking about it and I've decided to quit/ stop participating. It seems I'm not suited to this course.

Adam: You can't be serious. You can't stop trying now. Think of all the time you've invested.

Lynn: I know, I've thought of that but I don't think I have much choice.

Adam: Oh, that's not true! I don't agree! There're other options to just quitting/stop trying.

Lynn: Like what?

Adam: Well, maybe you could transfer to a course more suited to you.

Lynn: No. I've little or no chance of getting into another course now - it's too late. Besides, I'd prefer to continue with this course (to completion) if I'm going to do anything.

Adam: Well in that case, why don't you go and talk to your teacher. Say that you are going to work hard from now on and ask for some advice on how you can improve your assignment.

Lynn: Mm. I could do that. If I really work hard, I'm sure I could reach/achieve the required level in the work I've missed. I would like to pass/complete this course. OK I'll try.

Adam: That's a better idea.

Important note:
The language used in Conversation 2 (above) may seem easier to understand when compared with Conversation 1. However, the 'everyday' expressions used in Conversation 1 are used extensively by speakers of English. Therefore it is beneficial to become familiar with the everyday expressions used by the speakers in **Conversation 1**.

◀◀ **Replay Conversation 1**
Listen to the conversation again and fill in the missing words. You may have to listen more than once. (Don't worry about your spelling as this exercise focuses on listening skills - you can check your spelling later.)

Adam: How're you going?

Lynn: Oh, not very well really.

Adam: Why? **What's____**?

Lynn: Oh, it's this course I'm doing. I'm just **not_____ up.**

Adam: Well….

Lynn: I know, it's my fault. In the beginning I was **too laid-____**; thinking it would be **a piece of_____**. I didn't even **turn____ to** most classes. Well, I've just received my major assignment back and the teacher said it's **not up to_____** …and the way things are looking I'll probably fail.

Adam: So what're you going to do now?

Lynn: I've been thinking about it and I've decided to _____ **out**. It seems I'm **not _____ out for** this course.

Adam: You can't be serious. You can't _____ **in the towel** now. Think of all the time you've **put____.**

Lynn: I know, I've thought of that but I don't think I have much choice.

Adam: Oh **come on!** There're other options to just **giving____.**

Lynn: Like what?

Adam: Well, maybe you could transfer to a course more suited to you.

Lynn: No. I **don't____ a chance** of getting into another course now – it's too late. Besides, I'd prefer to _____ **this course through** if I'm going to do anything.

Adam: Well in that case, why don't you go and talk to your teacher. Say that you're going to **knuckle_____** from now on and ask for **some_____** on how you can improve your assignment.

Lynn: Mm. I could do that. If I really **get_____ into it,** I'm sure I could **catch_____** on the work I've missed. I would like to **get through** this course. OK I'll **give it a____.**

Adam: **That's more like it!**

> Now check your answers by comparing this page with CONVERSATION 1.

In order to become more familiar with these new everyday expressions:

◀◀ **Replay Conversation 1**
1) **Listen and tick the boxes ☑ next to the expressions as you hear them.**
2) **Write the definitions you can remember. (The first one has been done as an example.)**
   Check your answers with the reference list on page 120.

☐ What's up?..................................	*What is the problem?*
☐ not keeping up..........................	
☐ too laid-back............................	
☐ a piece of cake.........................	
☐ turn up to................................	
☐ not up to par............................	
☐ drop out	
☐ not cut out for..........................	
☐ throw in the towel......................	
☐ put in	
☐ Come on!.................................	
☐ giving up.................................	
☐ don't stand a chance............... ...	
☐ see (something) through..............	
☐ knuckle down...........................	
☐ some pointers...........................	
☐ get stuck into it........................	
☐ catch up..................................	
☐ get through..............................	
☐ give it a go...............................	
☐ That's more like it!	

LANGUAGE NOTE:

*The expression, *laid-back* means to be relaxed, but to be *__too laid-back__* can mean lazy and therefore has a negative meaning .

*The expression, *see (something) through* means to continue with a project although there are problems. We can also '*see a person through*' meaning help them in a difficult situation.

See notes on 'Come on!' on page 26.

CROSSWORD - LANGUAGE REVISION

Complete the sentences, choosing from the expressions or words listed below. You can use the clues in brackets ( ) at the end of each sentence to help you.

Then complete the crossword using the everyday expressions you have written.

The first one has been done as an example. You can check your answers on page 109.

~~not up to par~~	keep up	turn up	not cut out for	get through	piece of cake	
catch up	get stuck into it	throw in the towel	pointers	knuckle down	give up	

ACROSS

1) I'm sorry, this work is **_not up to par_**. You'll have to do it again. (not of an acceptable level)

3) I prefer to do outside work. I'm _____ _____ _____ _____ office work. (not suited to)

5) How do you manage to _____ ___ with all your school assignments and work part time too? (progress at the expected rate)

7) You have almost finished your course, so don't _____ ___ now. (stop trying)

9) The examination was a _____ ___ _____. I didn't have any problems at all. (an easy task)

11) If I _____ _____ _____ ___, I'll finish my work by lunchtime. (work hard).

DOWN

2) I failed my driving test last time, so I hope I _____ _____ it this time. (pass)

4) I've missed a lot of lessons, so I'll have to work hard to _____ ___ with the class. (reach the required level)

6) When the team lost the tenth game, the coach decided to _____ ___ ___ _____. (quit)

8) If you want to learn English quickly, it's important to _____ ___ to every class. (attend)

10) If you want travel next year, you'll have to _____ _____ and save some money. (work hard)

12) The travel agent gave us some _____ on travelling around South America. (advice)

FOCUS ON SPOKEN LANGUAGE

A) Giving suggestions

◄◄ Replay Conversation 1

Listen to Conversation 1 again and notice the expressions Adam used when giving suggestions to his friend. As you listen, complete the following two suggestions Adam gave Lynn.

Suggestion 1) 'Well, _____transfer to a course more suitable for you.'

Suggestion 2) 'Well in that case,_____go and talk to your teacher.'

The following sentences are all ways of giving suggestions. Which do you think is the strongest or most direct suggestion? Which is the least direct? Write number 1 next to the most direct suggestion; then 2, 3, 4 to show the order of less direct suggestions.

☐ Why don't you go and talk to your teacher?

☐ You should go and talk to your teacher.

☐ Go and talk to your teacher.

☐ Well, maybe you could go and talk to your teacher.

Check your answers on page 109.

B) Giving reasons

In Conversation 1, when Adam suggested that Lynn could transfer to a more suitable course, Lynn gave more than one reason for not doing so. Complete the following section from the conversation by writing in the expression Lynn used to introduce her second reason.

"No. I **don't stand a chance** of getting into another course now – it's too late. _____,
I'd prefer to **see this course through** if I'm going to do anything."

'**Besides**' means 'in addition to this ' or 'as well as this' and is often used in spoken English to give an additional reason for something. This expression is used in spoken, rather than formal written English. (**See information on 'Discourse markers' on page 53**.)

For example: 'I don't think I'll go to the cinema tonight. I'm very tired. **Besides**, there's a good movie on TV.'

Practice

In your notebook, or on the lines below, write several reasons for studying English.
Use 'besides' to add your final reason.

*I'm studying English because*_____

_____

_____

_____

C) Exclamations and the use of intonation

Exclamations are short expressions used to show an emotion, such as disbelief, encouragement or surprise. Exclamations are shown in written English with the symbol **!** which is called an exclamation mark. For example, 'Good luck!', 'I don't believe it!', 'Oh, come on!', 'At last!' are exclamations. In spoken English, in addition to the actual words used, speakers also indicate their *attitude* by using intonation.

Intonation refers to the rise and fall in the pitch or tone of the voice of a speaker. By using different intonation patterns, the same words can produce a different attitude or different meaning.

For example, the expression, 'Oh, come on!' spoken with rising intonation is used by the speaker in Conversation 1 to express strong surprise and/or disbelief.

The same expression can be spoken with falling intonation to express impatience.

'Oh, come on!' (meaning 'Hurry!')

When speakers uses a flat or level intonation it can convey lack of interest.

Look at these examples: Why? (checking/showing interest) Why! (impatience), Why? (lack of interest)

Note that intonation patterns are <u>always</u> related to the context in which they are used and individual speakers vary in their use of intonation. Some general guidelines are provided on the opposite page.

Practice: Using intonation to convey attitude

Imagine you are talking on the telephone. Try using different intonation to produce a different meaning for the following expression. Decide whether you would use rising, falling or level intonation for each situation below.

'Really?' - to show strong interest and surprise in what someone is saying and to show that you want to know more.

'Really?' - to show that you are <u>not</u> interested in what someone is saying and want to end the conversation.

Note that in face to face communication, the appropriate body language and facial expressions are also necessary to convey a particular attitude.

LANGUAGE NOTE:
In Conversation 1, when Adam suggested: 'There are other options to just giving up.'
Lynn replied: 'Like what?'

In this situation, 'Like what?' is an informal expression meaning, 'Give me some examples.'

Look at the following example: Lee: 'We'll have to buy some things for the party on Saturday.
Kim: 'Like what?'

The expression, 'Like what?' is not generally used in formal situations, as it could sound too abrupt.

Reference page
Understanding the use of intonation in spoken English

Intonation refers to the way the voice goes up and down in pitch when we are speaking. In English, speakers use intonation in various ways to convey meaning. As intonation is always related to the context in which it is used, it is *not* possible to give a 'rule' which applies in every situation. However, some general guidelines are given below with examples.

Falling intonation is mainly associated with:

* Introducing a topic with questions beginning with, *Who, When, Where, Why, What, How*

eg. *What does 'intonation' mean? Why is it so important?*

* 'Telling' new information or facts, making statements

eg. *'Intonation refers to the rise and fall in pitch when we are speaking.'*

Rising intonation is mainly associated with:

* Checking or enquiring further about information already mentioned.
This can be done by <u>repeating</u> information with rising intonation: eg. *Tomorrow?*

or

by asking a further question with rising intonation eg. *Is it arriving on Friday?*

* Showing interest or surprise in what has been said: eg. *Really?*

* Offering assistance eg. *Can I help you?*

When giving alternatives

* In utterances where two or more choices or alternatives are given, intonation generally rises on the first choice/s or alternative/s, then falls on the final item to show that the speaker is finished.

eg. *Would you prefer tea, coffee or a cold drink?*

When giving lists of items:

When listing items, intonation generally rises on the first item/s, then falls on the final item to show that the speaker is finished.

eg. *You'll need to buy pens, pencils and a dictionary.*

You can learn more about the intonation patterns of English in the book,
'Understanding English Pronunciation - an integrated practice course'.
See details on the back cover of this book.

UNIT 3

TALKING ABOUT EMPLOYMENT

Before you listen to the following conversation about employment, match the words in the box with the correct meaning listed below. You can check your answers on page 110.

résumé (also CV)	abilities		maintenance	qualifications
	relevant	handyman	first aid	supervisor

skills and talents (things you can do) _____
summary of education and work experience _____
emergency medical treatment _____
training and educational accomplishments _____
the work of keeping things in good condition _____
manager _____
related to the subject receiving attention _____
a person who does household repairs _____

(at an employment agency)

Listening for general understanding

Listen to the conversation between Mr White, who is seeking employment, and an employment agent. (Unit 3 on the audio recording.) The conversation contains everyday expressions that will be explained later in the unit – so don't worry if you don't understand every word. This time you are only listening for a general understanding of the topic.

As you listen, tick the correct answers below. (There may be more than one correct answer.) When you have finished you can check your answers on page 110.

1) Mr White is looking for a job because:

    a) he's just returned from a working holiday*

    b) he has just come out of hospital

2) Previously Mr White had worked as:

    a) a travel agent

    b) a maintenance worker

    c) an office worker

    d) a taxi driver

3) His other skills and qualifications include:

    a) a current driver's licence

    b) first aid certificate

    c) a nursing diploma

4) The employment agent suggests that Mr White should:

    a) improve his résumé.

    b) do a computer course.

    c) write a letter of application.

*In North American English, a 'working holiday' would be called a 'working vacation'.

Now, we'll look at the everyday expressions used in the conversation – turn to the next page.

CONVERSATION 1 (with everyday expressions)

◄◄ **Replay Conversation 1**
Read this conversation as you listen to the audio recording. Do you know what the _underlined_ **words mean? They are colloquial or 'everyday' expressions.**

Interviewer: OK Mr. White, I've **looked over** your résumé and I'd like to **go over** a few details with you before we proceed any further. I see you've just come back from overseas.

Mr. White: Yes, I was away for about a year on a working holiday. I had a variety of different jobs.

Interviewer: Yes, I see you've written 'handyman' on the form but what did you do specifically?

Mr. White: Well, as I said I had a number of jobs because I was travelling around. I did a bit of maintenance work…you know repairing things, painting - oh and some gardening.

Interviewer: I see. Well you need to **enlarge on** those skills in your résumé. Don't **take for granted** that an employer who reads your résumé will know what you mean by 'handyman'. You need to **spell out** your abilities and experience clearly so that they **stand out**. Remember you need to **sell yourself**.

Mr. White: Yes, I see what you mean.

Interviewer: OK. Let's take a look at your other qualifications. You have a background in accountancy and general office duties. Are you hoping to find **something along the same lines** again?

Mr. White: Actually, if possible I'd prefer to **keep going** with some sort of outdoor work rather than office work.

Interviewer: Mm. Let's see what we have here. Well, **it just so happens** there is a job available at the hospital for a maintenance supervisor. I **take it** you have a current driver's licence?

Mr. White: Yes, and I also have a first aid certificate which I did before I went overseas. I thought it might **come in handy** when looking for work.

Interviewer: Good. That's always **a plus**. Well it looks like you may **fit the bill** but you need to bring your résumé **up to date** and adapt it to fit this job, highlighting the relevant information…and you'll need to **put together** a letter of application too.

Mr. White: OK. I'll do that this afternoon. Could you tell me what salary I could **be looking at**?

Interviewer: It depends on experience **and so on**. I'll **look into it** before I **set up** an interview.

Mr. White: OK, that's great. Thanks.

Interviewer: In the meantime, you need to work on your résumé. Oh, and it would be a good idea to **brush up on** your first aid too. You may be asked questions about it at the interview.

Mr. White: Good idea! I'm probably a bit **rusty**.

Now let's see what the underlined expressions mean - look at the next page.

CONVERSATION 2 (explanation of everyday expressions)

Compare Conversation 1 with Conversation 2 -You will see that some of the words are different but the meaning is the same in both conversations. Find the underlined words in Conversation 1, then underline the words with the same meaning in Conversation 2. For example: *looked over* (Conversation 1) = *examined* (Conversation 2)

Interviewer: OK Mr. White, I've <u>examined</u> your résumé and I'd like to review/discuss a few details with you before we proceed any further. I see you've just come back from overseas.

Mr. White: Yes, I was away for about a year on a working holiday. I had a variety of different jobs.

Interviewer: Yes, I see you've written 'handyman' on the form but what did you do specifically?

Mr. White: Well, as I said I had a number of jobs because I was travelling around. I did a bit of maintenance work…you know repairing things, painting - oh and some gardening.

Interviewer: I see. Well you need to explain (those skills) in more detail in your résumé. Don't assume/suppose that an employer who reads your résumé will know what you mean by 'handyman'. You need to clearly explain your abilities and experience clearly so that they are noticeable. Remember you need to promote your value (as an employee).

Mr. White: Yes, I see what you mean.

Interviewer: OK. Let's take a look at your other qualifications. You have a background in accountancy and general office duties. Are you hoping to find something similar again?

Mr. White: Actually, if possible I'd prefer to continue with some sort of outdoor work rather than office work.

Interviewer: Mm. Let's see what we have here. Well… by chance there is a job available at the hospital for a maintenance supervisor. I suppose you have a current driver's licence?

Mr. White: Yes and I also have a first aid certificate which I did before I went overseas. I thought it might be useful when looking for work.

Interviewer: Good. That's always an advantage. Well it looks like you may be exactly the right person for the position but you need to change your résumé to include the most recent information and adapt it to fit this job, highlighting the relevant information …and you'll need to compose a letter of application too.

Mr. White: OK. I'll do that this afternoon. Could you tell me what salary I could expect?

Interviewer: It depends on experience and other things. I'll check/investigate before I arrange an interview.

Mr. White: OK, that's great. Thanks.

Interviewer: In the meantime, you need to work on your résumé. Oh, and it would be a good idea to revise your first aid too. You may be asked questions about it at the interview.

Mr. White: Good idea! I'm probably a bit weak/impaired due to lack of practice.

Important note:
The language used in Conversation 2 (above) may seem easier to understand when compared with Conversation 1. However, the 'everyday' expressions used in Conversation 1 are used extensively by speakers of English. Therefore it is beneficial to become familiar with the everyday expressions used by the speakers in **Conversation 1**.

◄◄ Replay Conversation 1
Listen to the conversation again and fill in the missing words. You may have to listen more than once. (Don't worry about your spelling as this exercise focuses on listening skills - you can check your spelling later.)

Interviewer: OK, Mr White, I've **looked** _____ your résumé and I'd like to ____ **over** a few details with you before we proceed any further. I see you've just come back from overseas.

Mr. White: Yes, I was away for about a year on a working holiday. I had a variety of different jobs.

Interviewer: Yes, I see you've written 'handyman' on the form but what did you do specifically?

Mr. White: Well, as I said I had a number of jobs because I was travelling around. I did a bit of maintenance work…you know repairing things, painting - oh and some gardening.

Interviewer: I see. Well you need to **enlarge** _____ those skills in your résumé. Don't _____ **for granted** that an employer who reads your résumé will know what you mean by 'handyman'. You need to _____ **out** your abilities and experience clearly so that they _____ **out**. Remember you need to _____ **yourself**.

Mr. White: Yes, I see what you mean.

Interviewer: OK. Let's take a look at your other qualifications. You have a background in accountancy and general office duties. Are you hoping to find **something along the same** _____ again?

Mr. White: Actually, if possible I'd prefer to **keep going** with some sort of outdoor work rather than office work.

Interviewer: Mm. Let's see what we have here. Well... **it just so** _____ there is a job available at the hospital for a maintenance supervisor. I **take it** you have a current driver's licence?

Mr. White: Yes and I also have a first aid certificate which I did before I went overseas. I thought it might **come in** _____ when looking for work.

Interviewer: Good. That's always **a plus**. Well it looks like you may _____ **the bill** but you need to bring your résumé ____ **to date** and adapt it to fit this job, highlighting the relevant information…and you'll need to _____ **together** a letter of application too.

Mr. White: OK. I'll do that this afternoon. Could you tell me what salary I could **be** _____ **at**?

Interviewer: It depends on experience **and** ____ **on**. I'll **look into it** before I **set** ____ an interview.

Mr. White: OK, that's great. Thanks.

Interviewer: In the meantime, you need to work on your résumé. Oh, and it would be a good idea to _____ **up on** your first aid too. You may be asked questions about it at the interview

Mr. White: Good idea! I'm probably a bit _____.

Now check your answers by comparing this page with CONVERSATION 1.

In order to become more familiar with these new everyday expressions:

◀◀ **Replay Conversation 1**
1) **Listen and tick the boxes ☑ next to the expressions as you hear them.**
2) **Write the definitions you can remember. (The first one has been done as an example.)**
   Check your answers with the reference list on page 121.

☐ looked over (something)	_examined_
☐ go over (something)....................	
☐ enlarge on (something)................	
☐ take for granted........................	
☐ spell out................................	
☐ stand out................................	
☐ sell yourself............................	
☐ something along the same lines........	
☐ keep going..............................	
☐ it just so happens.......................	
☐ take it...................................	
☐ come in handy..........................	
☐ a plus...................................	
☐ fit the bill..............................	
☐ bring something up to date...........	
☐ put together............................	
☐ (be) looking at.........................	
☐ and so on...............................	
☐ look into it.............................	
☐ set up...................................	
☐ brush up on............................	
☐ rusty....................................	

CULTURAL NOTE:
It is appropriate to ask an _employment agent_ about salary expectations, as Mr. White did in Conversation 1. However, remember that at a _job interview,_ your main aim is to convince your interviewer that you are the best person for the job. So, although it is not inappropriate to ask about salary, do so only after you have promoted yourself and your ability to do the job well. Remember a job interview is your opportunity to 'sell yourself'.

CROSSWORD - LANGUAGE REVISION

Complete the sentences, choosing from the everyday expressions in the box below.
You can use the clues in brackets ( ) at the end of each sentence to help you.
Then complete the crossword using the everyday expressions you have written.
The first one has been done as an example. You can check your answers on page 110.

sell yourself	along the same lines	go over	~~fit the bill~~	a plus	stand out
	enlarged on	take for granted	spells out	brush up on	

ACROSS

1) I think I ___fit the bill___ for this nursing job that's advertised in the paper. I have all the qualifications and experience they require. (am the right person for the job)
3) It's important to _____ _____ at a job interview and show that you are the best person for the job. (promote your value and assets)
5) When I finish school, I'd like to do something _____ _____ _____ _____ as my brother. He really enjoys his work in advertising. (similar to)
7) My office is very close to the railway station which is __ _____ because I don't like driving in peak hour traffic. (an advantage)
9) We'll ___ _____ the plans for our trip again next week, just before we leave (review/discuss)

DOWN

2) My boss always _____ _____ exactly how he wants things done so that there are no problems later. (clearly explains)
4) My teacher doesn't _____ _____ _____ that we know what she means. She always checks by asking questions. (assume/suppose)
6) I'll have to _____ ____ ____ my Italian before we go to Rome at the end of the year, as I've promised to be the guide! (revise/review)
8) Today, our teacher _____ ___ the lecture he gave last week. This time I understood everything much better. (explained in more detail)
10) It's a good idea to highlight the most important words in a different colour so they _____ _____ (are noticeable)

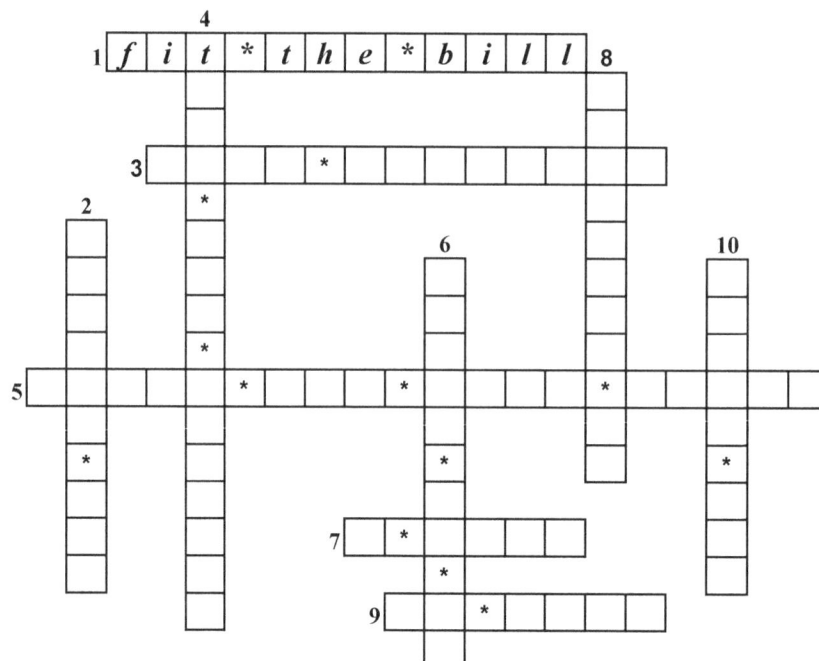

Answers, page 110.

FOCUS ON SPOKEN LANGUAGE

A) The use of 'articles' - a, an, the

Words such as *a, an, the* are called *articles*. Students of English often have problems knowing when to use articles. This may be because they are usually pronounced as *unstressed* sounds in spoken language and as a result, are difficult to hear. In this unit you will practise listening to the pronunciation of articles and look at the pattern of their use.

How are articles used?

Articles are used before nouns (eg. *the* interview) or noun groups (eg. *a* working holiday). Look at Conversation 1 again (page 32) and **highlight the articles** (a, an, the) in different colours so that you can analyse the different ways they are used.

- *a/an* are called *indefinite articles* because they are used:

a) when we are **not definite** (specific) about *which* thing, place, time or person.

   eg. 'I was away for about *a* year on *a* working holiday.'

b) when we talk about something for the first time in our conversation.

   eg. 'I have *a* first aid certificate. I'll set up *an* interview.'

c) before expressions of quantity. eg. 'I'd like to go over *a* few details.'

The following examples have been taken from Conversation 1 of this unit.

article	thing (noun or noun group)
a	few details
a	year
a	working holiday
a	variety of different jobs
a	good idea

article	thing (noun)
an	*e*mployer
an	*i*nterview

Note: __an__ is used before vowel sounds.

- *the* is called the *definite article* because it is used:

a) when it is clear from the context *which* thing the speakers are taking about.

   eg. I see you've written handyman on *the* form.

b) when we talk about *definite* (specific) things. eg. There's a job available at *the* hospital.

c) when we talk about things which have been mentioned previously in the conversation.

   eg. You may be asked questions about your qualifications at *the* interview.

Look at the pattern. The following examples have been taken from Conversation 1 of this unit.

article	thing (noun)	reason for using the definite article
the	form	It is clear from the context *which* 'form' the speaker is talking about.
the	hospital	As there is usually one main hospital in a town, 'the hospital' is specific.
the	interview	The 'interview' has been mentioned previously in the conversation.

- *No article* is used when talking about things in <u>general</u>.

   eg. 'I enjoy gardening.' (not *the* gardening)
   'I'd prefer outdoor work.' (not *the* outdoor work)

B) Pronunciation - Listening Practice

In Unit 1, the weak, unstressed pronunciation
of articles '*a*', '*an*', '*the*' was examined.

◀◀ **Replay Conversation 1**
Listen to Conversation 1 again and notice the *weak, unstressed* pronunciation of *a*, *an*, *the*.

> Note: When '**the**' comes before a word with an initial vowel sound, as in 'th<u>e</u> <u>i</u>nterview' at the
> end of Conversation 1, '**the**' is pronounced with a long vowel sound, as in the word 'th<u>e</u>se'.

C) Talking about the past using 'present perfect' and 'simple past' tenses.

In spoken (and written) language we indicate time (past, present, future) through **verb tenses**.

In Conversation 1 of this unit, several tenses have been used by the speakers. Let's see how the **present perfect** and **simple past tense** are used in the conversation to talk about the past.

Look at this example:

> Interviewer: ...I see you**'ve** just **come back** from overseas.
> Mr. White: Yes, I **was** away for about a year on a working holiday. I **had** a variety of different jobs.
> Interviewer: Yes, I see that you**'ve written** 'handyman' on the form but what **did** you **do** specifically?
> Mr. White: ...I **had** a number of jobs.....I **did** a bit of maintenance work...

Look at the pattern:

Interviewer's comments, introduced with **present perfect tense**	Mr White's reply, using **past simple tense**
I see you'**ve** just **come back** from overseas. ('ve = have)	Yes, I **was** away for about a year.
I see that you'**ve written** 'handyman' on the form.....	I **had** a number of jobs... I **did** a bit of maintenance work...

The present perfect tense consists of **have (or has)** + **past participle**, eg. have <u>come</u>, have <u>written</u>.

- In spoken language, contracted forms are used. (eg. you*'ve* come; you*'ve* written; she*'s* been)

General Guidelines

- We use the **present perfect tense** to show a connection between the past and the present; to show that the past action/event is relevant at the time of speaking. We usually *don't give a specific time* when the past event/action occurred. eg. 'I*'ve been* to Europe.'

- We use the **past simple tense** to talk about completed events/actions; often saying *when* the event happened. eg. 'I *went* to Europe *last year*.'

When introducing a topic about the past in a general way (not referring to specific time) English speakers use the *present perfect tense*. Then, when continuing to talk about the same topic, giving more detail, speakers use the *simple past tense*.

Practice

The following questions and answers may be heard at a job interview. Complete the questions and answers, adding suitable present perfect and past simple tenses.

When you have finished, you can check your answers on page 110.

present perfect tense	past simple tense
Have you *completed* your training yet?	Yes, I _____ my course in 2003.
_____ you *used* this computer program before?	No, I _____ another program in my last job.
_____ you _____ in a shoe factory before?	Yes, I _____ in a big shoe factory in Taiwan.
_____ you _____ this type of machine before?	Yes, I *operated* one like this in my last job.

See information on forming past tense verbs on page 38 and 39.
See Unit 6, Part 6 A (page 71) for other ways of talking about the past.

D) Interview strategies - giving informative answers at an interview

At the beginning of Conversation 1, while discussing Mr. White's résumé, the interviewer said, '*I see you've just come back from overseas*'. This was a request for more information.

◄◄ Replay Conversation 1

Listen to Mr White's reply (Conversation 1, line 3) and notice that, rather than simply replying 'Yes', Mr. White gave an informative answer. Write his informative reply on the line below.

Mr White: _____

Later in the interview, when the interviewer said, '*I take it you have a current driver's licence?*' Mr. White again gave an informative reply, giving more details about himself, rather than just saying, 'Yes'.

Look at the pattern:

Request for information:		**Informative reply:**
I see you	*'ve just come back* from overseas.	Yes, I was away for about a year on a working holiday. I had a variety of jobs.
I take it you	*have* a current driver's licence.	Yes, and I also have a first aid certificate which I did before I went overseas. I thought it may come in handy when looking for work

Remember! When someone uses the expressions, '*I see you + verb…*' or '*I take it you + verb...*', they are often seeking more details about you and the topic of conversation.

> REMEMBER
> An interview presents a good opportunity to give more details on your experience,
> skills and qualifications so be prepared to give informative answers,
> rather than simple 'yes'/'no' replies.

Practice – Interview Strategies

Imagine you are at a job interview and an interviewer
is looking at your resume and asking questions.
Look at the questions below and give a reply with an
informative answer to each question (not just 'yes' or 'no').

Interviewer: I see from your résumé that you have been studying English?

You: _____

Interviewer: I see you've had some experience doing similar work in the past?

You: _____

Interviewer: I take it you are happy to do some training?

_____

Information about English verbs

A verb is a word that shows **action** (eg. ran, go, work)
state   (eg. is, am, were)
experience (eg. like, feel).

English verbs may consist of one or more words. Auxiliary (or 'helper') verbs are used together
with other verbs to form tenses, questions and other expressions. The principal auxiliary verbs
are **be, is, am, are**, **have, has** and **do**.

For example: auxiliary   main
verbs   verb

John	is	enjoying his new job.
She	has	finished her course.
We	don't	want to fail our exam, of course.
They	are	opening a new agency soon.

Forming past tense verbs

The letters '**ed**' are added to most verbs to form a past simple tense or past participle.
eg. work → work**ed** → (have) work**ed;** follow → follow**ed** → (have) follow**ed**

However, for some verbs, the spelling is *irregular* (doesn't follow the usual rules).
For example: see → saw → (have) seen.   See the example list on the following page.

Note: The verb '*have*' is used in a variety of ways in English. See page 104 for details.

Reference page
A list of some irregular verbs

base verb infinitive present simple	past simple	past participle for the present perfect tense, use with *have/has*
be/am/is/are	was/were	been
beat	beat	beaten
become	became	become
begin	began	begun
bend	bent	bent
bite	bit	bitten
blow	blew	blown
break	broke	broken
bring	brought	brought
build	built	built
burn	burned/burnt	burned/burnt
buy	bought	bought
catch	caught	caught
choose	chose	chosen
come	came	come
dig	dug	dug
do	did	done
draw	drew	drawn
drink	drank	drunk
drive	drove	driven
eat	ate	eaten
fall	fell	fallen
feed	fed	fed
feel	felt	felt
fight	fought	fought
find	found	found
fly	flew	flown
forget	forgot	forgotten
forgive	forgave	forgiven
get	got	got (US=gotten)
give	gave	given
go	went	gone
grow	grew	grown
have	had	had
hear	heard	heard
hide	hid	hidden
hold	held	held
keep	kept	kept
know	knew	known
lay	laid	laid
lead	led	led
leave	left	left

base verb infinitive present simple	past simple	past participle for the present perfect tense, use with *have/has*
lend	lent	lent
light	lit	lit
lose	lost	lost
make	made	made
mean	meant	meant
meet	met	met
pay	paid	paid
read /ri:d/	read /red/	read /red/
ride	rode	ridden
ring	rang	rung
rise	rose	risen
run	ran	run
say	said	said
see	saw	seen
sell	sold	sold
send	sent	sent
show	showed	shown
sing	sang	sung
sink	sank	sunk
sit	sat	sat
sleep	slept	slept
speak	spoke	spoken
spell	spelt/spelled	spelt/spelled
spend	spent	spent
spring	sprang	sprung
stand	stood	stood
steal	stole	stolen
sting	stung	stung
swear	swore	sworn
swim	swam	swum
swing	swung	swung
take	took	taken
teach	taught	taught
tear /teə(r)/	tore	torn
tell	told	told
think	thought	thought
throw	threw	thrown
understand	understood	understood
wake	woke	woken
wear	wore	worn
win	won	won
write	wrote	written

(Units 1 - 3)

This section reviews some of the expressions that were introduced in Units 1, 2, and 3 and gives you a chance to see what you have remembered.

- Look at the pictures on the opposite page and decide what the people are saying by choosing from the expressions below.

- Match each picture with an appropriate expression by writing the correct letter in the box next to each expression.

- For extra practice, you could write the appropriate expression in the space provided in the picture.

1) 'I'm brushing up on the geography of Asia.' ☐

2) 'Could you enlarge on your plans for this area, please.' ☐

3) 'You'll really have to knuckle down, if you want to get through the course.' ☐

4) 'I wouldn't count on getting the washing dry today.' ☐

5) 'We don't stand a chance of getting a parking place here!' ☐

6) 'Take this. It'll come in handy if it rains.' ☐

7) 'I'm sorry. You've missed the boat. It's already been sold.' ☐

8) 'I'm not cut out for all this exercise.' ☐

9) 'I'd like something along the same lines as this one.' ☐

(Answers: page 111)

UNIT 4

TECHNOLOGY AND BUSINESS

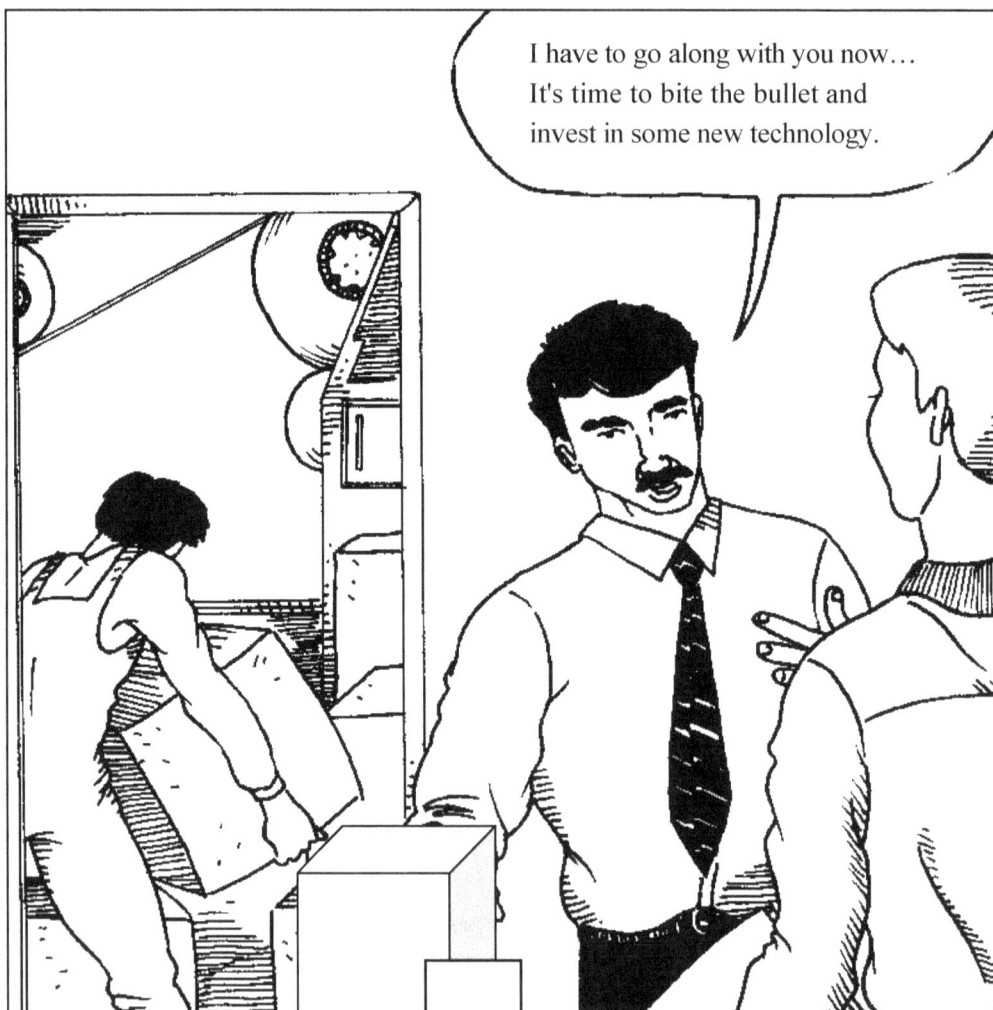

We live in a fast changing world. Think about the changes that you have seen taking place in different aspects of life during the last twenty years.

In this unit you will listen to a conversation about changes in technology and business. Before you listen, match the following words with the correct meaning below.

changeover	slave	industry	costly

a person controlled by someone/something _____   change to a new system   _____

a branch of production/manufacture   _____   expensive/costing a lot of money _____

Listening for general understanding

Now listen to this conversation in which the manager of a company is talking to his assistant about making changes in the business. The conversation contains everyday expressions which will be explained later in the unit - so don't worry if you don't understand every word. This time you are only listening for a general understanding of the topic. As you listen, tick the correct answers below.

1) The Manager wants to talk to Kim, his assistant, because:

    a) business is improving.

    b) business is not going well.

2) The industry they are working in is:

    a) the music industry.

    b) the printing industry.

    c) the toy making industry.

3) The manager has decided to:

    a) invest in some better technology.

    b) move the business to another factory.

    c) apply for a better job.

4) The manager:

    a) is happy about changing technology.

    b) thinks things are changing too quickly.

You can check your answers on page 111.

Now, we'll look at the everyday expressions used in the conversation – turn to the next page.

CONVERSATION 1 (with everyday expressions)

◄◄ **Replay Conversation 1**
Read this conversation as you listen to the audio recording. Do you know what the
underlined **words mean? They are colloquial or 'everyday' expressions.**

Manager: Oh Kim! Do you have a minute? I'd like to discuss a few things with you… As you know, sales have been **falling off** over the past few months and **between you and me**, things aren't looking very good.

Assistant: Well...

Manager: Look, before you say anything, I'm not **pointing the finger** at you. I know you've suggested several times that we need to **go in for** better equipment, if we're going **hold our own** in the industry. And I have to **go along with** you now; it's time to **bite the bullet** and invest in some better technology.

Assistant: That's great news. I'm sure it's the right move.

Manager: Well, as you've pointed out, we're **up against** some strong competition in the printing industry and a lot of small businesses are **folding**. If we don't **jump on the bandwagon** now, we could very likely **go under** as well.

Assistant: I agree, absolutely. The thing is, you have to be **at the cutting edge** of change, if you want to stay in business these days.

Manager: That's for sure… You know, I've been **putting off** making the changes because I know it'll be costly, not only in equipment, but in training too. But **the bottom line** is if we don't spend money, we won't make any.

Assistant: That's very true. So when do you think we'll start the changeover?

Manager: **The sooner the better**, I suppose. There're some big changes to make and I'm not really looking forward to them. You know ... I wonder whether all this new technology is really making our lives easier. It seems to me we've created **a vicious circle**...

Assistant: What do you mean?

Manager: Well, technology's supposed to have given us more time and freedom but it seems we've become slaves to technology.

Assistant: Mm. I hadn't thought of it that way.

Manager: But then maybe I just don't like change... It's **mind-boggling** the way technology is changing! No sooner do I **get my head around** something new, than it changes again!

Assistant: Well, I know what you mean but I think we have to **go with the flow,** whether we like it or not.

Manager: I suppose so. Well, I'd better **get the ball rolling**. I'll start making some phone calls now.

Now let's see what these expressions mean - look at the next page.

CONVERSATION 2 (explanation of everyday expressions)

*Compare Conversation 1 with Conversation 2 -*You will see that some of the words are different but the meaning is the same in both conversations. Find the underlined words in Conversation 1, then underline the words with the same meaning in Conversation 2. For example: *falling off* (Conversation 1) = *decreasing* (Conversation 2)

Manager: Oh Kim! Do you have a minute? I'd like to discuss a few things with you .... As you know, sales have been <u>decreasing</u> over the past few months and this information is private (so don't tell anyone), things aren't looking very good.

Assistant: Well.....

Manager: Look, before you say anything, I'm not saying the problem was caused by you. I know you've suggested several times that we need to get/seek better equipment if we're going to keep/defend our position in the industry. And I have to agree with you now; it's time to make an important/difficult decision and invest in some better technology.

Assistant: That's great news. I'm sure it's the right move.

Manager: Well, as you've pointed out, we're competing with some strong competition in the printing industry and a lot of small businesses are failing/closing. If we don't follow the popular course now, we could very likely fail as well.

Assistant: I agree, absolutely. The thing is, you have to be involved in the most advanced/recent developments of change, if you want to stay in business these days.

Manager: That's for sure… You know, I've been delaying making the changes because I know it'll be costly, not only in equipment, but in training too. But the basic truth is, if we don't spend money, we won't make any.

Assistant: That's very true. So when do you think we'll start the changeover?

Manager: As soon as possible, I suppose. There're some big changes to make and I'm not really looking forward to them. You know ... I wonder whether all this new technology is really making our lives easier. It seems to me we've created a cycle of problems in which the solution to one problem, makes more problems.

Assistant: What do you mean?

Manager: Well, technology's supposed to have given us more time and freedom but it seems we've become slaves to technology.

Assistant: Mm. I hadn't thought of it that way.

Manager: But then maybe I just don't like change...It's amazing/unbelievable the way technology is changing! No sooner do I understand/accept something new, than it changes again!

Assistant: Well, I know what you mean but I think we have to accept and progress with changes (in life) whether we like it or not.

Manager: I suppose so. Well, I'd better start the project/activity. I'll start making some phone calls now.

Important note:
The language used in Conversation 2 (above) may seem easier to understand when compared with Conversation 1. However, the 'everyday' expressions used in Conversation 1 are used extensively by speakers of English. Therefore it is beneficial to become familiar with the everyday expressions used by the speakers in **Conversation 1**.

◀◀ Replay Conversation 1
Listen to the conversation again and fill in the missing words. You may have to listen more than once. (Don't worry about your spelling as this exercise focuses on listening skills - you can check your spelling later.)

Manager: Oh Kim! Do you have a minute? I'd like to discuss a few things with you .... As you know, sales have been _____ **off** over the past few months and _____ **you and me**, things aren't looking very good.

Assistant: Well.....

Manager: Look, before you say anything, I'm not **pointing the** _____ at you. I know you've suggested several times that we need to **go in for** better equipment if we're going to **hold our** _____ in the industry. And I have to _____ **along with** you now; it's time to _____ **the bullet** and invest in some better technology.

Assistant: That's great news. I'm sure it's the right move.

Manager: Well, as you've pointed out, we're _____ **against** some strong competition in the printing industry and a lot of small businesses are **folding**. If we don't _____ **on the bandwagon** now, we could very likely **go** _____ as well.

Assistant: I agree, absolutely. The thing is, you have to be **at the cutting edge** of change, if you want to stay in business these days.

Manager: That's for sure… You know, I've been **putting** _____ making the changes because I know it'll be costly, not only in equipment, but in training too. But **the bottom** _____ is, if we don't spend money, we won't make any.

Assistant: That's very true. So when do you think we'll start the changeover?

Manager: **The sooner the** _____, I suppose. There're some big changes to make and I'm not really looking forward to them. You know ... I wonder whether all this new technology is really making our lives easier. It seems to me we've created **a vicious** _____...

Assistant: What do you mean?

Manager: Well, technology's supposed to have given us more time and freedom but it seems we've become slaves to technology.

Assistant: Mm. I hadn't thought of it that way.

Manager: But then maybe I just don't like change...It's _____ -**boggling** the way technology is changing! No sooner do I **get my head** _____ something new, than it changes again!

Assistant: Well, I know what you mean but I think we have to _____ **with the flow**, whether we like it or not.

Manager: I suppose so. Well, I'd better **get the** _____ **rolling**. I'll start making some phone calls now.

> Now check your answers by comparing this page with CONVERSATION 1.

In order to become more familiar with these new everyday expressions:

◄◄ **Replay Conversation 1**

1) Listen and tick the boxes ✓ next to the expressions as you hear them.

2) Write the definitions you can remember. (The first one has been done as an example.)
   Check your answers with the reference list on page 122.

☐ falling off ....……………… *decreasing* _____

☐ between you and me ....….… _____

☐ pointing the finger.……………… _____

☐ go in for.…………………..….…… _____

☐ *hold our own..……………...…..... _____

☐ go along with.…………….…...….. _____

☐ bite the bullet...…………….…….. _____

☐ up against ……………….…...….. _____

☐ folding…….......….……….……… _____

☐ jump on the bandwagon....….…… _____

☐ go under.……………………....….. _____

☐ *(be) at the cutting edge...…......… _____

☐ *putting off...…....……………...… _____

☐ the bottom line.…………….…..… _____

☐ the sooner the better....…………... _____

☐ a vicious circle.……………....….… _____

☐ *mind-boggling...……………...…..… _____

☐ get my head around.………….…….. _____

☐ go with the flow.………………….. _____

☐ get the ball rolling....……………..…. _____

LANGUAGE NOTES:

* The expression '*hold our own*' can also be expressed using other pronouns.
   eg. 'hold *your* own' (keep/defend *your* position), 'hold *her* own' (keep *her* position) etc.

* '*at the cutting edge*' can also be expressed as, '*on the cutting edge*'.

* '*put off*' (postpone) can be used before a noun phrase, (eg. Don't *put off* your next appointment).
   We can also say, 'Don't *put* the appointment *off*.' When used with a pronoun, the pronoun
   goes in the middle of the expression. eg. Don't *put* it *off*. (See **Book 1**, Unit 9, Part 6D for details)

* We say something is '*mind-boggling*' when we think it is amazing, strange or difficult
   to understand. We also say that something '*boggles the mind*'.

CROSSWORD - LANGUAGE REVISION

Complete the sentences, choosing from the everyday expressions that are listed below.
You can use the clues in brackets ( ) at the end of each sentence to help you.
Then complete the crossword using the everyday expressions you have written.
The first one has been done as an example. Answers, page 111.

hold your own	cutting edge	go in for	mind boggling	vicious circle	get the ball rolling
go under	point the finger	up against	put off	bottom line	bandwagon

ACROSS

1) Our business will ***go under***, if our sales don't improve soon. (fail/ close)
3) Don't worry. With your excellent service and cheaper prices, you will ____ _____ _____ when the new shopping centre opens. (keep your position)
5) I can't _____ ____ going to the dentist any longer, my tooth is aching badly. (delay)
7) Most businesses have a web-page now and we should jump on the _____ too. (follow the popular course)
9) The scientists who made the new discovery were at the _____ _____ of research. (involved in the most recent developments)
11) We'll have to ____ ____ _____ _____ today, if we are going to finish the job by next week. (start the project)

DOWN

2) Some people _____ ____ _____ at the government for the increase in crime. (blame)
4) He was ___ _____some good players, but he won the competition. (competing with)
6) It is _____ _____ to think that life may exist on other planets. (amazing)
8) The _____ _____ is that many businesses fail if they don't plan for the future. (basic truth)
10) The economy has created a _____ _____ . There are less jobs because people aren't spending money. People aren't spending money because the economy isn't creating jobs. (a cycle of problems)
12) We are leaders in our industry because we ___ ___ _____ the most recent equipment as soon as its available on the market. (get/show interest in)

FOCUS ON SPOKEN LANGUAGE
A) Hearing and pronouncing syllables correctly - Revision

In *Understanding Spoken English - Book One*, practice in hearing and pronouncing syllables correctly was provided. The following section of this unit revises this aspect of spoken English.

- Spoken words are formed with syllables (or units of sound).
- A syllable is formed when individual sounds are pronounced together to form one unit of unbroken sound within a word.
- A word may contain one or more syllables.
  For example: *come* = one syllable; *welcome* = two syllables; *unwelcome* = three syllables

It's important to be able to **hear** how many syllables a word contains in order to be able to **pronounce** it correctly.

Listening practice

◄◄ Replay Conversation 1

- Listen to the first part of Conversation 1 (printed below) again. As you listen, decide how many syllables the underlined words contain.

- Write the number of syllables contained in each word above the words. The first one has been done as an example. Pause the recording while you write your answer. You can check your answers on page 111.

2

Manager: Oh Kim! Do you have a **minute**? I'd like to **discuss** a few things with you.... As you

know, **sales** have been falling off over the past few **months**...and **between** you and me,

things **aren't** looking very **good**.

Assistant: Well.....

Manager: Look, **before** you say **anything**, I'm not pointing the **finger** at you. I know you've

suggested **several** times that we need to go in for better **equipment** if we're going to

hold our own in the **industry**. And I have to go **along** with you now. It's time to bite

the bullet and **invest** in some better **technology**.

Note: The word 'several' can be pronounced as two or three syllables. eg. sev(e)ral
      However, when spoken quickly as in Conversation 1, it is pronounced as two syllables.

Hearing and pronouncing syllables correctly

In words with more than one syllable, one syllable is usually spoken more clearly and strongly than the others. Knowing and using correct stress in words is essential to correct pronunciation.

Stress refers to the strongest (primary) syllable in words of more than one syllable. For example, in the word '**ind**ustry', the first syllable has the primary stress; in the word 'tech**no**logy' the second syllable has the primary stress.

Important Note

A good dictionary will provide very useful information on how to pronounce words correctly. At the beginning of your dictionary, near the Pronunciation Key, you will see an explanation of how **word stress** is shown on all words listed in the dictionary.

Dictionaries use various symbols to show which syllable should be stressed, so it's important to check which symbol **your** dictionary uses. For example, in the word 'eleven' (which contains three syllables), the stress is on the second syllable. Look at the way this may be shown in a dictionary.

*some dictionaries show a stress mark **' before and above** the stressed syllable.   eg. **'sev**en
*some dictionaries show a stress mark **' after and above** the stressed syllable.   eg. sev'en
*some dictionaries use **a line under** the stressed syllable, to show the stressed part. eg. <u>sev</u>en

To avoid confusion, always check which symbol your dictionary uses.

How does **your** dictionary show that the first syllable is stressed in the word *seven*? _____

Pronunciation can affect meaning

Correct pronunciation of a word involves stressing the correct syllable, as incorrect stress can sometimes change the meaning of a word.

For example, the word 'minute' can have two meanings
depending on which syllable is stressed.

<u>mi</u>nute (with stress on the first syllable) is a noun which means 'sixty seconds'

mi<u>nute</u> (with stress on the second syllable) is an adjective which means 'very, very small'.

Dictionary Practice

Using your dictionary, check the following two syllable words and underline the stressed syllable in each word. Notice how different stress patterns can change the meaning.

meaning	meaning
discus (noun) *round, flat object thrown in sports events*	discuss (verb) *to talk about something*
rebel (noun) _____	rebel (verb) _____
present (noun)_____	present (verb) _____
object (noun) _____	object (verb) _____

You can check your answers on page 111.

Note: For more information and practice in hearing and pronouncing syllables correctly, see the book, *'Understanding English Pronunciation – an integrated practice course'*.
See details on the back cover of this book.

B) Using adjectives ending with 'ed' or 'ing'

In Conversation 1, the speaker described the changes in technology as *mind-boggling*.

eg. 'It's *mind-boggling* the way technology is changing!' (Conversation1, line 26)
    In this sentence, *mind-boggling* is used as an adjective.

When talking about experiences or feelings, we can use words ending in *ing* (eg. It was excit*ing*) or words ending in *ed* (eg. I was excit*ed*).

It is very important to use *ed* or *ing* adjectives correctly to convey the correct meaning. For example: '*I am bored* (not interested)', conveys a very different meaning to, '*I am boring* (I make other people feel uninterested and tired)'.

1) Look at the explanation and examples, then complete the exercises below:

To describe **how we (or other people) are affected** or **how we feel about** something, we end the word with *ed*. eg. '**I am confused** by this form.'	To describe **the person, thing or situation** which **gives the effect** to us (or other people), we end the word with *ing*. eg. '**This form** is **confusing**'.
1a) She was amaz**ed** by the story.	1b) The story was amaz**ing**.
2a) I feel relax**ed** at the beach.	2b) The beach is relax**ing**.
3a) I get bor**ed** at school.	3b) I think school is _____.
4a) I get _____ when I study for too long.	4b) It's tir**ing** to study for too long.
5a) I was _____ by the movie.	5b) The movie was frighten**ing**.
6a) I get excit**ed** when I watch soccer.	6b) I think soccer is an _____ game.
7a) I am annoy**ed** by her letter.	7b) Her letter is _____.

2) Complete the story below using the correct words from the box.

tired	tiring	exciting	excited	interesting	amazed	boring	bored	amazing

The sports competition was very _____. Everyone in the audience was cheering

and clapping. We were all very _____ when the winner was announced. I was

_____ to see how fast the competitors could run. Their speeds were _____.

Unfortunately, the speeches that followed the competition were a bit _____. I usually

get _____ when people keep talking for a long time. In fact, I started to feel so _____

I had trouble keeping my eyes open. It had been a very _____ but _____ day.

Note: In grammar books, verbs ending in *ed* are called *past participles;* verbs ending in *ing* are called *present participles*. However, when *describing* something, as in the examples on this page, they act as *adjectives*. eg. This is a *boring* lesson. The class is *bored*.

C) Discourse markers in spoken language

In spoken language, speakers use various expressions to show connection between what has been said before and what is going to be said next.

For example:

- Expressions such as *'but'* or *'on the other hand',* introduce **a contrasting idea.**
- Expressions like, *'I suppose..', 'I think..',* indicate that the speaker is going to give **an opinion**.
- Some expressions are used to *focus attention* on what will be said next. eg. *'Well, in fact ...'*

Look at the following section from Conversation 1. Notice the expressions that the speakers use to *focus attention* on what they are going to say next.

Assistant: I agree, absolutely. **The thing is**, you have to be at the cutting edge of change, if you want to stay in business these days.

Manager: That's for sure… **You know**, I've been putting off making the changes because I know it'll be costly, not only in equipment, but in training too. **But the bottom line is**, if we don't spend money, we won't make any.

Expressions like these are sometimes called *discourse markers.* They are an important part of everyday conversation, as they give signals about the kind of information that will come next.

Various expressions also *show the attitude of the speaker* to what they are talking about.

- Listen to the following section from Conversation 1 and fill in the missing expressions.

- What do the expressions show about the Manager's *attitude* to changing technology?

Assistant: …. So when do you think we'll start the changeover?

Manager: The sooner the better, _____. There're some big changes to make and I'm not really looking forward to them. You know .... _____ whether all this new technology is really making our lives easier. _____ that we've created a vicious circle......

Assistant: What do you mean?

Manager: Well, technology's supposed to have given us more time and freedom but _____ we're becoming slaves to technology.....

Answers, page 112.

Expressions like, *'I suppose...', 'I wonder..', 'it seems...',* as well as introducing a personal opinion, give the impression that the manager may be a little apprehensive or uncertain about changes in technology and business.

Reference page - Discourse markers or Connectors

'Discourse' refers to a stretch of written or spoken language that is longer than a sentence. Discourse markers are expressions we use to show connection between what has already been said (or written) and what we will say (or write) next.

In spoken English, discourse markers also indicate the **attitude of the speaker** to what has been said, what is being said and prepare the listener for what will be said next. Some examples are given below.

More informal	More formal
general conversation	speeches, lectures, reports

Introducing an opinion

As far as I'm concerned, ...	*In my opinion, ...*
If you ask me, ...	*It seems...*
In my opinion...	

Focussing attention

The main thing is....	*An important point is...*
Let's face it!	*It is important to realise...*
As a matter of fact,	*In fact...*
You know...	*With regard to...*
Speaking of...	*With reference to...*

Clarifying information

What I mean is...	*In other words,*
That is to say...	

Generalising

As a rule...	*In most cases...*
On the whole...	*In general, ...*
...and so on	*...etcetera*

Changing the subject

By the way,	*On a different subject...*
While I think of it...	

Adding information

..on top of that	*In addition...*
and what's more...	*Furthermore...*
Besides...	*Additionally,*

Summarising or concluding

To cut a long story short...	*In summary,*
And in the end...	*In conclusion,*

As noted in the introduction, our choice of words and expressions is always dependent on the context or situation in which it is used. Therefore, when learning a new language, it is necessary for students to become familiar with the different contexts in which certain expressions are used before beginning to use them in their own speech.

UNIT 5

A NEW VENTURE - MAKING DECISIONS

What's the most important decision you have ever made? Did you have to think about it for a long time before you made your decision? Before making important decisions, people often think about the *pros and cons* involved. In other words, they consider the advantages and disadvantages of the venture. In this unit you will hear expressions related to decision making.

Listening for general understanding

Listen to this conversation between friends who are talking about a new venture. The conversation contains colloquial or everyday expressions that will be explained later in the unit - so don't worry if you don't understand every word. This time you are only listening for a general understanding of the topic. As you listen, tick the correct answers below. (There may be more than one correct answer.) When you have finished you can check your answers on page 112.

1) What kind of business would Don like to start?

        a) a video shop.
        b) a coffee shop.
        c) a camera shop.

2) Where is the business he is interested in buying?

        a) Highland Street.
        b) High Street.
        c) Brighten Street.

3) Don plans to promote the business by having:

        a) special introductory prices.
        b) an 'Under New Management' sign.
        c) a party.

4) Kara suggests that before making a decision Don should:

        a) go to the bank.
        b) talk to his father
        c) write a list of the pros and cons.

Now, we'll look at the everyday expressions used in the conversation – turn to the next page.

CONVERSATION 1 (with everyday expressions)

◀◀ Replay Conversation 1
Read this conversation as you listen to the audio recording. Do you know what the _underlined_ **words mean? They are colloquial or 'everyday' expressions.**

Don: You know how I've been **toying with the idea** of starting my own coffee shop.

Kara: Yes, you've been talking about it for as long as I can remember.

Don: Well, the other day I was looking through the newspaper and I **came across** one for sale. It's the one on High Street; you know, near the corner. It's **going for a song**. I'm seriously thinking about **taking the plunge** and buying it.

Kara: But I thought you wanted to start a business **from scratch**.

Don: Well, I did. But buying one that's already **up and running** would make it easier. It'd save a lot of time, money and hard work.

Kara: Mm, not necessarily. I heard **through the grapevine** that the business was **going downhill** and that's why they're trying to **get rid of** it.

Don: Yes, I know it's a bit **run-down** but a bit of **elbow grease** will fix that and I have a few ideas **up my sleeve** to get the new business **off the ground**. I'll put up a big sign saying, 'Under New Management', and I'll have special introductory prices to bring in the customers. I think it'll go well.

Kara: Maybe, maybe not. Look, I'm not trying to **talk you out of it**. I just wouldn't want to see you **getting your fingers burned**. If I were you, I'd write a list of the **pros and cons** of starting a business **from scratch** or buying one that's already established and **weigh up** the possibilities on both sides before making your decision.

Don: Yes, that's a good idea. Don't worry. I know there's a lot to **take into account**. I'll **look into it** a lot more before I make a final decision. I know there're **drawbacks** on both sides but I'll **do my homework** before I **go ahead** with anything.

Kara: And you'll let me know if there's anything I can do to help, won't you.

Don: Yes. I will, thanks.

Now let's see what the underlined expressions mean - look at the next page.

CONVERSATION 2 (explanation of everyday expressions)

Compare Conversation 1 with Conversation 2 -You will see that some of the words are different but the meaning is the same in both conversations. Find the underlined words in Conversation 1, then underline the words with the same meaning in Conversation 2. For example: *toying with the idea* (Conversation 1) = *thinking about* (Conversation 2)

Don: You know how I've been <u>thinking about</u> starting my own coffee shop.

Kara: Yes, you've been talking about it for as long as I can remember.

Don: Well, the other day I was looking through the newspaper and I (by chance) found one for sale. It's the one on High Street; you know, near the corner. It's being sold very cheaply. I'm seriously thinking about taking the important step and buying it.

Kara: But I thought you wanted to start a business from the beginning (without help).

Don: Well, I did. But buying one that's already operating would make it easier. It'd save me a lot of time, money and hard work.

Kara: Mm, not necessarily. I heard through information from other people that the business was not doing well and that's why they're trying to dispose of it.

Don: Yes, I know it's a bit neglected/in a bad condition but a bit of hard work will fix that and I have a few ideas in my mind to get the new business into successful operation. I'll put up a big sign saying, 'Under New Management', and I'll have special introductory prices to bring in the customers. I think it'll go well.

Kara: Maybe, maybe not. Look, I'm not trying to tell you not to do it. I just wouldn't want to see you have a bad experience. I were you, I'd write a list of the advantages and disadvantages of starting a business from the beginning or buying one that's already established and consider the possibilities on both sides before making your decision.

Don: Yes, that's a good idea. Don't worry. I know there's a lot to consider. I'll investigate a lot more before I make a final decision. I know there are disadvantages on both sides but I'll research and check information before I continue with anything.

Kara: And you'll let me know if there's anything I can do to help, won't you.

Don: Yes. I will, thanks.

Important note:
The language used in Conversation 2 (above) may seem easier to understand when compared with Conversation 1. However, the 'everyday' expressions in Conversation 1 are used extensively by speakers of English. Therefore it is beneficial to become familiar with the everyday expressions used by the speakers in **Conversation 1**.

◀◀**Replay Conversation 1**
Listen to the conversation again and fill in the missing words. You may have to listen more than once. (Don't worry about your spelling as this exercise focuses on listening skills - you can check your spelling later.)

Don: You know how I've been **toying with the** _____ of starting my own coffee shop.

Kara: Yes, you've been talking about it for as long as I can remember.

Don: Well, the other day I was looking through the newspaper and I _____ **across** one for

        sale. It's the one on High Street; you know, near the corner. It's **going for a** _____.

        I'm seriously thinking about **taking the** _____ and buying it.

Kara: But I thought you wanted to start a business **from** _____.

Don: Well, I did. But buying one that's already _____ **and running** would make it easier.

        It'd save me a lot of time, money and hard work.

Kara: Mm, not necessarily. I heard **through the** _____ that the business was **going** _____

        and that's why they're trying to **get rid of** it.

Don: Yes, I know it's a bit **run-down** but a bit of _____ **grease** will fix that and I have a

        few ideas **up my** _____ to get the new business **off the** _____. I'll put up a big sign

        saying, 'Under New Management', and I'll have special introductory prices to bring in

        the customers. I think it'll go well.

Kara: Maybe, maybe not. Look, I'm not trying to **talk you** _____ **of it.** I just wouldn't want to

        see you **getting your** _____ **burned**. If I were you, I'd write a list of the **pros and cons**

        of starting a business from scratch or buying one that's already established and **weigh up**

        the possibilities on both sides before making your decision.

Don: Yes, that's a good idea. Don't worry. I know there's a lot to _____ **into account**.

        I'll **look** _____ **it** a lot more before I make a final decision. I know there are **drawbacks**

        on both sides but I'll **do my homework** before I _____ **ahead** with anything.

Kara: And you'll let me know if there's anything I can do to help, won't you.

Don: Yes. I will, thanks.

Now check your answers by comparing this page with
CONVERSATION 1.

In order to become more familiar with these new everyday expressions:

◀◀ **Replay Conversation 1**
1) **Listen and tick the boxes** ☑ **next to the expressions as you hear them.**
2) **Write the definitions you can remember. (The first one has been done as an example.)**
   Check your answers with the reference list on page 123.

☐	toying with the idea…………………….	*examined*
☐	came across…………………………….	
☐	going for a song……………………….	
☐	taking the plunge………………………..	
☐	from scratch……………………………..	
☐	up and running…………………………..	
☐	*through the grapevine………………..	
☐	going downhill………………………….	
☐	get rid of………………………………..	
☐	run-down………………………………..	
☐	elbow grease……………………………	
☐	up my sleeve…………………………..	
☐	get (the new business) off the ground	
☐	talk you out of………………………..	
☐	*getting (your) fingers burnt……..……	
☐	pros and cons………………………….	
☐	weigh up ………………………………	
☐	take into account……………………..	
☐	look into it……………………………..	
☐	drawbacks…………………………….	
☐	do (my) homework…………………..	
☐	go ahead…………………………….…	

LANGUAGE NOTE:
To hear something '**through the grapevine**' usually means that the information has come through several people before it has been told to you. We can also say '**on the grapevine**'.

The expression '**get your fingers burned**' often refers to bad experiences, usually involving money. Note: **burned** can be also be written as '**burnt**'.

CROSSWORD - LANGUAGE REVISION

Complete the sentences, choosing from the everyday expressions which are listed below.
You can use the clues in brackets ( ) at the end of each sentence to help you.
Then complete the crossword using the everyday expressions you have written.

up and running	~~come across~~	elbow grease	look into	toying with the idea
going for a song	off the ground	through the grapevine		get your fingers burned
	weigh up	take the plunge	pros and cons	

ACROSS

1) Let me know if you ***come across*** a set of keys. I've lost my car keys. (find by chance)
3) I've decided to _____ _____ _____ and go to university. (take the important step)
5) Take care when buying a second-hand car. Don't _____ _____ _____ _____.
   (have a bad experience)
7) It's important to _____ ____ the pros and cons before making big decisions. (consider)
9) I'm _____ _____ _____ _____ of buying a new car soon. (thinking about)
11) I heard _____ _____ _____ that he is leaving. (through information heard from
   other people)

DOWN

2) I'll write a list of the _____ _____ _____ before I decide. (advantages and disadvantages)
4) It's important to _____ _____ any new venture carefully before proceeding. (investigate)
6) There's a lot of work to do before our business gets ____ _____ _____ (into successful operation)
8) I bought this car because it was _____ _____ __ _____. I hope it goes well. (very cheap)
10) Our new business will be ____ _____ _____ in a few weeks. (operating).
12) We'll need a lot of _____ _____ to clean this oven. It's very dirty. (effort/hard work)

Answers, page 113.

FOCUS ON SPOKEN LANGUAGE
A) Using pronouns in place of nouns

Pronouns (words such as *I, you, they, she, him, we, it, etc.*) are used in English in the place of *previously mentioned names or things (nouns)*. In English, to repeat the name continually sounds very unnatural. In spoken English, pronouns are generally used to refer to a previously mentioned noun.

For example, we **don't** say: 'Where's the **car**? The **car** should be in the driveway but the **car**'s not there'

rather, we **use pronouns to refer to the previously mentioned noun:**

'Where's the **car**? **It** should be in the driveway but **it**'s not there.'

In this section, the use of *it* and *one* is examined. Look at the following section from Conversation 1.

> Don: You know how I've been toying with the idea of starting my own coffee shop.
>
> Kara: Yes, you've been talking about *it* for as long as I can remember.
>
> Don: Well, the other day I was looking through the newspaper and I came across *one* for sale. *It*'s the *one* on High Street; you know, near the corner. *It*'s going for a song. I'm seriously thinking about taking the plunge and buying *it*.

What do the __underlined__ words '*it*' and '*one*' refer to?
The first sentence has been done as an example.

1) 'Yes, you've been talking about *it* for as long as I can remember'.

   '*it*' refers to __*the idea of buying a coffee shop*__.

2) I came across *one* for sale.

   '*one*' refers to _____

3) '*It*'s the *one* on High Street; you know, near the corner'.

   '*It*' refers to _____ '*one*' refers to_____

4) '*It*'s going for a song. I'm seriously thinking about taking the plunge and buying *it*'.

   '*It*' refers to _____   Answers, page 113.

B) Giving Advice

When giving advice, we often use the pattern, '**If I were you, I would + verb…**'
eg. '**If I were you, I'd go** to the doctor for a check up'.

Note that the contracted form **'d** is often used in spoken language (rather than **would**).
In Conversation 1, Kara gives Don some advice using this pattern.
Find and complete the following sentence from Conversation 1 (page 56).

> 'If I were you, _____
> _____or buying one that's already established and weigh up the possibilities on
> both sides before making any decisions.'
>
> Answer, page 113.

We use the pattern, '**If I were you, I would** when we want to be polite (not too dogmatic), when making suggestions.

This kind of sentence has two parts:

The part with **if + past tense verb**, and the part with **would + base verb (present simple)**
For example: ▼   ▼   ▼   ▼

| **If** I **were** you, | I **would write** a list of the pros and cons. |

Notice that a **past tense verb** is used, though this sentence is referring to the **future**.
Using a **past tense verb** with '**if**' makes the sentence less dogmatic/more polite.

Note: '*If I was you, ...*' is also used when giving advice, however, '*If I were you,*' is more usual.

We also use this pattern in the **negative** form (would**n't**).

| *eg. If* I *were* you, I *wouldn't go* without an umbrella. |

C) Talking about future possibilities

When we are trying to make a decision, we often talk about the **possible** results of a particular action. In other words, we say what is likely to happen, **if** we do a particular thing.
In these situations we use **would + base verb**. For example:

'I think it **would be** better to buy a new car rather than a second hand one.
It **would save** money on repairs'.

Look at the following sentence from Conversation 1,
in which Don talks about the possible advantages of buying
the coffee shop on High Street.

| Don: ......'But buying one that's already up and running **would make** it easier.' |

Don uses **would + base verb** in another sentence to talk about future possibilities.
Complete the following sentence from Conversation 1 (page 56).

| 'It | and hard work.' |

D) Using 'a lot of' and 'a bit of' used with uncountable nouns

'a lot of'
In spoken English, the expression 'a lot of' can be used with countable and uncountable nouns.
An 'uncountable' noun is one that has no plural form. Some commonly used uncountable nouns are:

| information, knowledge, advice, news, work, homework, research, help, water, rain, ice, heat, noise, glass, petrol, gas, oil, grease, tea, coffee, sugar, money |
| **See page 105 for more information on uncountable nouns.** |

In Conversation 1, Don uses the expression 'a lot of' with uncountable nouns, when he is explaining why he wants to buy the coffee shop business on High Street.
Check Conversation 1, (page 56) and complete the following sentence:

Don: …But buying one that's already up and running would make it easier.

It'd save me **a lot of** _____ .

'a bit of'

Don uses the expression 'a bit of' with an uncountable noun when he talks about what he'll need to use to fix the 'run-down' condition of the coffee shop. '*A bit of*' means '*a small amount*' or '*some*'.
Check Conversation 1, (page 56) and complete the following sentence:

Don: Yes, I know it's a bit run-down but
_____ will fix that.

Note: In the expression 'a bit run-down' - '*a bit*' (without *of*) is used with an adjective to mean '*slightly*' or '*a little*'.

With countable nouns, 'a bit of ' is followed by 'a' or 'an'.
eg. We have **a bit of a problem**.

'a lot'

'a lot' (without 'of') can be used before an infinitive to mean 'many things'. eg. There's <u>a lot</u> <u>to do</u>.

infinitive

Check Conversation 1 (page 56), then complete the following sentence with '**a lot**' + **infinitive**.

Don: …Don't worry. I know there's _____

'a lot' (without 'of') is used before an adjective or adverb to give emphasis to a statement.

eg.   He can run **a lot faster** than anyone!

We need **a lot more** than we have now!

She's **a lot older** than she looks!

I'll try **a lot harder** next time.

I'll look into it _____
before I make a final decision.

Check Conversation 1, (page 56)
and complete the sentence in the illustration:

Answers, page 113

UNIT 6

TALKING ABOUT
THE PAST

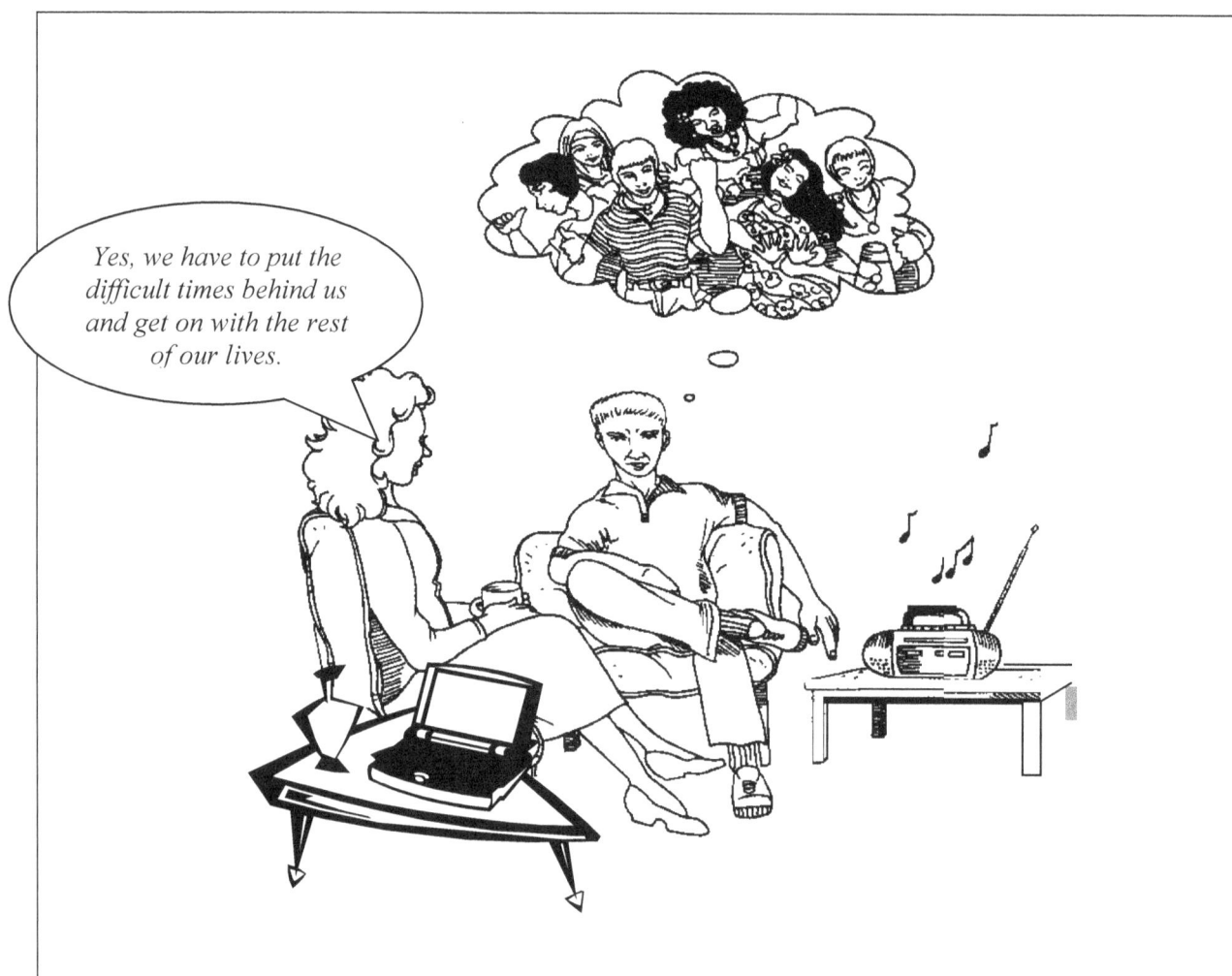

In this unit you will hear someone talking about good memories, as well as a difficult situation in the past. In English there is an expression, 'Every cloud has a silver lining'. This means that every bad situation has some positive aspect. Do you agree with this expression?

Before you listen to the conversation, match the words in the box with the correct meanings below. You can check your answers on page 114.

| a shock | experiences | mischief | bitter | recover | independent |

playful but unacceptable conduct _____   unhappy/angry because of problems _____

a sudden, bad experience _____   improve/return to a good situation _____

being able to support yourself _____   things that happen to us during life _____

Listening for general understanding

Listen to the following conversation in which friends, who are working together, are talking about the past. (Unit 6 on the audio recording.) The conversation contains 'everyday' expressions that will be explained later in the unit - so don't worry if you don't understand every word. This time you are listening for a general understanding of the topic. As you listen, tick the correct answers below. When you have finished you can check your answers on page 114.

1) When Dan (first speaker) was younger, he used to:

    a) party all weekend.

    b) work seven days a week.

    c) sleep most of the weekend.

2) One day he received the terrible news that:

    a) his parents had been killed in an accident.

    b) his friends had been killed in an accident.

    c) his grandmother had died.

3) Dan told his friend that:

    a) he had learned a lot from his experiences.

    b) he would never recover from his experience.

Now, we'll look at the everyday expressions used in the conversation – turn to the next page.

CONVERSATION 1 (with everyday expressions)

◄◄ **Replay Conversation 1**
Read this conversation as you listen to the audio recording. Do you know what the _underlined_ words mean? They are colloquial or 'everyday' expressions.

Dan: You know, whenever I hear that song, it **takes me back to** my younger days…
We used to **get into** some mischief. **It's a wonder** I'm still **in one piece**!

Eve: What did you use to do?

Dan: We had a lot of fun but we did some **crazy** things! We used to **burn the candle at both ends** most weekends. We'd party all night and go straight to work the next day without any sleep.....or we'd drive across the country for the weekend **on the spur of the moment**.

Eve: Really? How long did you **keep that up**?

Dan: Oh, quite a while. I'd probably have kept it up a lot longer if my life hadn't been **turned upside down** one day by some terrible news.

Eve: Why? What happened to change things?

Dan: Well, I was at work one day when I received the news that my parents had been killed in a car accident.

Eve: Oh no, that's terrible. I'm so sorry. You haven't talked about that before. It must have been a terrible shock.

Dan: Yes, it was. It took me a long time to **get over it** and I was very bitter for a while.... But **I'd rather not go into it** now.

Eve: Mm. Well, you don't **strike me as** a bitter person now.

Dan: No, because one day someone said to me, 'We can let our experiences in life make us bitter or better' and I thought to myself, 'It's time to **put this behind me** and **get on with** the rest of my life.' And you know I **haven't looked back** since then.

Eve: That's great.

Dan: Of course, I wish things had **turned out** differently. But you know I learned a lot from that difficult time in my life. I learned to **stand on my own feet** and that we never know what's **around the corner**, so we should try to **make the most of** every day.

Eve: Yes, that's very true.

Now let's see what these expressions mean - look at the next page.

CONVERSATION 2 (explanation of everyday expressions)

Compare Conversation 1 with Conversation 2 -You will see that some of the words are different but the meaning is the same in both conversations. Find the underlined words in Conversation 1, then underline the words with the same meaning in Conversation 2. For example: *takes me back to* (Conversation 1) = *makes me remember* (Conversation 2)

Dan: You know, whenever I hear that song, it makes me remember my younger days…
We used to be involved in some mischief. I'm surprised I'm still alive and unharmed!

Eve: What did you use to do?

Dan: We had a lot of fun but we did some foolish (but exciting) things! We used to have very little sleep (because of too much activity) most weekends. We'd party all night and go straight to work the next day without any sleep...or we'd drive across the country for the weekend suddenly, without planning.

Eve: Really? How long did you continue (that activity)?

Dan: Oh, quite a while. I'd probably have kept it up a lot longer if my life hadn't been completely changed one day by some terrible news.

Eve: Why? What happened to change things?

Dan: Well, I was at work one day when I received the news that my parents had been killed in a car accident.

Eve: Oh no, that's terrible. I'm so sorry. You haven't talked about that before. It must have been a terrible shock.

Dan: Yes, it was. It took me a long time to recover and I was very bitter for a while ...But I'd rather not talk about/discuss it now.

Eve: Mm. Well, you don't seem/appear to me as a bitter person now.

Dan: No, because one day someone said to me, 'We can let our experiences in life make us bitter or better' and I thought to myself, 'It's time to recover from this unhappy experience and proceed with the rest of my life'. And you know I have progressed/succeeded since then.

Eve: That's great.

Dan: Of course, I wish things had had a different result/happened differently. But you know I learned a lot from that difficult time in my life. I learned to be independent and that we never know what's in the future, so we should try to fully use and enjoy every day.

Eve: Yes, that's very true.

Important note:
The language used in Conversation 2 (above) may seem easier to understand when compared with Conversation 1. However, the 'everyday' expressions used in Conversation 1 are used extensively by speakers of English. Therefore it is beneficial to become familiar with the everyday expressions used by the speakers in **Conversation 1**.

◀◀ **Replay Conversation 1**
Listen to the conversation again and fill in the missing words. You may have to listen more than once. (Don't worry about your spelling as this exercise focuses on listening skills - you can check your spelling later.)

Dan: You know, whenever I hear that song, it **takes me** _____ **to** my younger days… We used to **get into** some mischief. **It's a** _____ I'm still **in** _____ **piece**!

Eve: What did you use to do?

Dan: We had a lot of fun but we did some **crazy** things! We used to _____ **the candle at both ends** most weekends. We'd party all night and go straight to work the next day without any sleep...or we'd drive across the country for the weekend **on the spur of the** _____.

Eve: Really? How long did you _____ **that up**?

Dan: Oh, quite a while. I'd probably have kept it up a lot longer if my life hadn't been **turned upside** _____ one day by some terrible news.

Eve: Why? What happened to change things?

Dan: Well, I was at work one day when I received the news that my parents had been killed in a car accident.

Eve: Oh no, that's terrible. I'm so sorry. You haven't talked about that before. It must have been a terrible shock.

Dan: Yes, it was. It took me a long time to **get** _____ **it** and I was very bitter for a while.... But **I'd rather not go** _____ **it** now.

Eve: Mm. Well, you don't _____ **me as** a bitter person now.

Dan: No, because one day someone said to me, 'We can let our experiences in life make us bitter or better' and I thought to myself, 'It's time to **put this** _____ **me** and **get** _____ **with** the rest of my life'. And you know I **haven't** _____ **back** since then.

Eve: That's great.

Dan: Of course, I wish things had **turned** _____ differently. But you know I learned a lot from that difficult time in my life. I learned to **stand on my own** _____ and that we never know what's **around the** _____, so we should try to **make the** _____ **of** every day.

Eve: Yes, that's very true.

Now check your answers by comparing this page with
CONVERSATION 1.

In order to become more familiar with these new everyday expressions:

◀◀ **Replay Conversation 1**
1) **Listen and tick the boxes** ☑ **next to the expressions as you hear them.**
2) **Write the definitions you can remember. (The first one has been done as an example.)**
   Check your answers with the reference list on page 124.

☐ takes me back to........................... *makes me remember*

☐ to get into (some mischief)..............

☐ It's a wonder..........................

☐ in one piece...........................

☐ crazy..............................

☐ burn the candle at both ends...........

☐ on the spur of the moment.............

☐ *keep (that) up..........................

☐ *turned upside down....................

☐ get over it ....

☐ I'd rather not go into it.....…..........

☐ strike me as ....….....…......

☐ put this behind me........…....…......

☐ get on with (something)..............

☐ * haven't looked back..................

☐ turned out ....

☐ * stand on my own feet...............

☐ * around the corner....................

☐ make the most of ....

LANGUAGE NOTES

* '***Keep up***' can be used before nouns. eg. '***Keep up*** the good work!' (Continue the good work!)
  When '***keep up***' is used with pronouns, the pronoun goes in the middle of the expression.
  eg. '***Keep*** <u>it</u> ***up***!', 'I can't ***keep*** <u>this</u> ***up*** for three weeks!'

*When we say something '*has been **turned upside down**'* we usually mean '*has been changed
  in a **negative/disorderly way**'*.

*The expression, '*I have**n't** looked back',* is always expressed in the negative (***not/never***) but
  has a positive meaning: '*I have progressed/succeeded /gone forward*'

*'***Stand on my own feet***' can also be expressed as '*Stand on my own **two** feet*'

* We say something is '***just** around the corner*', meaning *in the **near** future or very soon.*
  eg. 'My wedding is ***just around the corner***.' = 'My wedding is ***very soon***.'

CROSSWORD - LANGUAGE REVISION

Complete the sentences, choosing from the everyday expressions listed below.
You can use the clues in brackets ( ) at the end of each sentence to help you.
Then complete the crossword using the everyday expressions you have written.

keep it up	in one piece	stand on my own feet	make the most of
get on with	spur of the moment	~~burn the candle at both ends~~	
put it behind	around the corner	takes me back	get over

ACROSS

1) If you ***burn the candle at both ends***, you won't get enough sleep and you could get sick. (have very little sleep because of too much activity)
3) 'I'm pleased to see you are exercising everyday. I hope you _____'.(continue)
5) She's lucky to be _____after her terrible car accident. (alive and unharmed)
7) Thanks for your help in the past but I can _____ now. (be independent)
9) Our annual business meeting is just _____, so we'd better start preparing. (in the near future)

DOWN

2) When we're on vacation, we like to do things on the _____ ___ ____ _____ (without planning)
4) When I look at these old photographs, it _____ ____ _____ to my time as a student.(makes me remember)
6) It's a great day! Let's _____ ____ _____ it by having a picnic by the river.(fully enjoy)
8) My vacation is over, so I'll have to _____ ____ _____ my studies now. (proceed with)
10) When I had a serious car accident, I thought I would never _____ _____ it. (recover)
12) I made a big mistake but now I'm trying to _____ ___ _____ me. (recover from it)

Answers, page 114.

FOCUS ON SPOKEN LANGUAGE

A) Talking about the past using 'used to' and 'would'.

When we talk about the past in English, we use different verb tenses to indicate how the past events we are talking about, relate to the present time. In this unit, you will see how we use *'used to'* or *'would'* to indicate *past habits or activities*.

- We use *'used to'* or *'would'* to talk about *a past habit or activity* which has since been *discontinued*; to indicate that things have *changed*. Look at these examples:
  'I *used to exercise* regularly', indicates, 'I don't exercise regularly now.' (Things have changed).
  'When I was single, I *would* go to clubs every night', means, 'I don't go to clubs every night now.'

- We use *'used to'* to talk about past *situations* as well as actions; to indicate how *a situation has changed*. For example: 'I *used to be* single.' (but now I'm married)
  'I *used to be* thin.' (but I'm not thin now)

- *Would* is used to talk about past habits or actions but is not used to talk about past situations.

---

1) Read Conversation 1 and note the things that Dan (and his friends) *used to do*. Complete the following sentences from Conversation 1 on page 66.

   We used to_____

   We used to_____

2) Find the things Dan (and his friends) *would do* in their younger days.
   Complete the following sentences. (Note that '*we would*' is spoken as *we'd*).

   We'd_____

   _____....or

   we'd _____

3) Does Dan still do those things? _____(Answers, page 114)

Notice the Pattern: *used to + (base form of verb)* and *would + (base form of verb)*

Look at these examples and note the pattern.

	(base form of verb)	
I *used to*	*walk*	regularly but now I catch the bus.
We *used to*	*do*	some crazy things when we were younger.
I *would*	*party*	all weekend when I was in my teens but now I stay home on weekends.
We'*d*	*drive*	across the country on the spur of the moment.

Practice

Think about how your life has changed. Complete the following sentence about your life. Remember we use *'used to + base form of verb'* or *'would + base form of verb'* to talk about past habits and activities which we have **discontinued** now.

When I was younger, I_____

_____

---

* See Unit 3, Part 6C for examples of other ways of indicating past time.

B) Pronunciation - Words ending in 'ed'
◀◀Replay Conversation 1

Listen to the second line of Conversation 1 and notice the word 'used'──▶
is pronounced as **one** syllable, not two syllables.
The '**ed**' ending is pronounced as /t/.

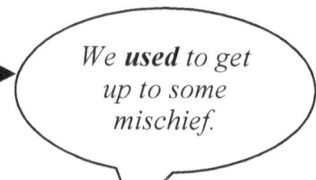

*We **used** to get up to some mischief.*

The letters '**ed**' at the end of words can be pronounced as
/t/, /d/, or /əd/ depending on the letters or sounds that come
before the letters '**ed**'.

As a general rule:

- '**ed**' is pronounced as /**t**/ after consonant sounds and/or letters
  such as **s, p, t, th, ch, k, sh**. For example: kick**ed** is pronounced /kɪk**t**/;
  miss**ed** is pronounced as /mɪs**t**/

- '**ed**' is pronounced as /**d**/ after consonant sounds such as **m, n, b, z, v, l.**
  For example: hemm**ed** is pronounced as /hem**d**/; sneez**ed** is pronounced /sneez**d**/

Practice 1

Look at this section from Conversation 1. Using the 'rules' above, put /d/ or /t/ above the words
in boxes as in the first example. Then **listen** to the section of Conversation 1 to check your answers.

	/**d**/
Eve:	Why, what happened to change things?
Dan:	Well, I was at work one day when I received the news that my parents had been killed in a car accident.
Eve:	Oh no, that's terrible. I'm so sorry. You haven't talked about that before. It must have been a terrible shock.

You can also check your answers on page 114.

- **ed** is pronounced as an extra syllable, /əd/, when added to words which end in /**d**/ or /**t**/.
  For example: When **ed** is added to the word **visit** - visi**ted** is pronounced visitəd (3 syllables)
  When **ed** is added to the word **end** - en**ded** is pronounced as endəd (2 syllables)

Practice 2

Put the following words in the correct column below. Check your answers on page 114.

~~loved~~	~~waited~~	*included*	*looked*	*worked*	*started*	*arrived*	*washed*

ed pronounced as /**d**/	**ed** pronounced as /**t**/	**ed** pronounced as /əd/
loved		*waited*

Note:
Some past tense verbs may be written with a 't' at the end, rather than 'ed' eg. learned/learnt, burned/burnt.

C) Pronouns in spoken English

In Unit 5 Part 6A the use of pronouns, in place of nouns, was examined. The following section will revise and extend that information.

Look at the first line of Conversation 1 below. What does the pronoun, 'it', refer to?

> Dan: You know, whenever I hear that song, **it** takes me back to my younger days…

Answer: 'it' refers to 'that song' or more specifically to 'the situation of hearing that song'.

Using the pronoun 'it' to refer to 'the present situation'

In spoken English, pronouns can be used to refer to something that is 'understood' between the speakers. The pronoun **'it'** can be used at the beginning of a sentence to refer to something that is understood by the speakers to mean **'the situation we are talking about'** or **'this situation'**.

Look at some examples:

'It's amazing!'	= 'The situation we are talking about is amazing.'
'It's clear he doesn't want to do the job.'	= 'The situation is clear. He doesn't want the job.'
'It's beautiful here, isn't it?'	= 'This situation is beautiful, isn't it?'

In Conversation 1 (page 66), the speaker says, 'It's a wonder I'm still in one piece!' This means: The situation (crazy things I did in my younger days) makes me surprised I'm still in one piece!

'This' and 'that' as pronouns

This and *that* can also be used in conversations to refer to something that is 'understood' between the speakers. For example: '**This** is fun!'; 'Who said **that**?'; '**That**'s very interesting!'

> *This* is generally used for people, things and situations that are close (in space or time) to the speaker.
>
> *That* generally refers to things and situations that are more distant (in space or time).

Practice

Refer to Conversation 1 (page 66) again to answer the following questions.
What do ' this' ' that' and 'it' refer to in each sentence?

1) 'How long did you keep **that** up?' (line 7)

   'that' refers to _____

2) '**It** must have been a terrible shock.' (line 13)

   'It' refers to _____

3) 'It's time to put **this** behind me and get on with the rest of my life'(line 19)

   'This' refers to _____ .

Check your answers on page 114.

(Units 4 - 6)

This section reviews some of the expressions that were introduced in Units 4, 5, and 6 and provides an opportunity to see what you have remembered.

- Look at the pictures on the opposite page and decide what the people are saying by choosing from the expressions below.

- Match each picture with an appropriate expression by writing the correct letter in the box next to each expression.

- For extra practice, you can write the appropriate expression in the space provided in the picture.

1) 'Between you and me, I can't get my head around this modern art.' ☐

2) 'I'm going to bite the bullet and apply for a business loan.' ☐

3) 'The universe is so vast. It's mind-boggling!' ☐

4) 'The doctor said, I won't look back if I keep up my medicine and exercise.' ☐

5) 'Look at this! It's going for a song!' ☐

6) 'I know it's run down but a bit of elbow grease will fix it.' ☐

7) 'I heard through the grapevine that they are getting engaged soon.' ☐

8) 'You must try to put this trouble behind you and get on with your life.' ☐

9) 'I want to weigh up the pros and cons before I go ahead with a booking.' ☐

(Answers: page 115)

UNIT 7

ASKING FOR DIRECTIONS

Have you ever tried to find your way around an unfamiliar city in busy traffic? It can be confusing! In the following conversation you will hear a person who is lost, asking someone for directions. Before you listen, put the words in the box next to the correct meaning listed below.

overpass	avoid	a bend	back streets

go around/stay away from _____

bridge over a road or railway _____

smaller/less busy streets _____

a curve/change in direction in a road _____

Answers, page 115.

Listening for general understanding

Now listen to this conversation in which a driver, who is trying to find his way through the city, asks someone for directions. The conversation contains 'everyday' expressions that will be explained later in the unit - so don't worry if you don't understand every word. This time you are listening for a general understanding of the topic. As you listen, tick the correct answers below. (There may be more than one correct answer.) When you have finished you can check your answers on page 120.

1) The driver wants to know the way to

      a) Fairmont
      b) Fairgrove
      c) Highgrove

2) The driver says:

      a) he's been in busy traffic for an hour
      b) the traffic has not been busy
      c) there are more one-way streets than before

3) Which of the following ways does the service station attendant suggest:

      a) the old road
      b) through the backstreets
      c) past the hospital

4) Which way does the driver say he will try?

      a) the old road
      b) the backstreets
      c) the highway
      d) past the hospital

Now, we'll look at the everyday expressions used in the conversation – turn to the next page.

CONVERSATION 1 (with everyday expressions)

◀◀ Replay Conversation 1
Read this conversation as you listen to the audio recording. Do you know what the _underlined_ words mean? They are colloquial or 'everyday' expressions.

Attendant:	Need some help?
Driver:	Yeah, I'm **after** some directions. Could you tell me the best way to Fairgrove, please?
Attendant:	Sure...now let me think which'd be the best way to go this time of the day. You'll come to **a bottleneck** if you go along the highway, so don't go that way.
Driver:	**Tell me about it!** We've been in **bumper to bumper traffic** for the last hour on the highway. The traffic's **backed up** to the first exit.
Attendant:	Oh, well there's probably been **a pile up** again if it's that bad.
Driver:	Mm. And they've put in a lot of one way streets since I was last here and it's completely **thrown me**. I couldn't **turn off** where I wanted to.
Attendant:	Yeah, it's a bit **tricky** around here now but there're a couple of ways you can go other than the highway. You could avoid the city completely by taking the old road. I'll show you on the map there. See…see here.
Driver:	Yes I see...on the other side of the highway.
Attendant:	That's right. **Watch out for** the trucks on that road though… it winds quite a bit so it can get a bit **hairy**; especially this time of day when the truck drivers are trying to avoid the traffic too.
Driver:	OK. I'll **keep that in mind**.
Attendant:	Your other option is to go through the back streets. It is **a short cut** but you won't avoid the traffic completely. Do a U-turn here and then take the second on the right back there.
Driver:	You mean back there, near the park?
Attendant:	That's right. Turn right there. Go through two sets of lights. Take the next left and you'll come to a bend in the road. Follow that through, go over the overpass and you'll see signs to Fairgrove. Once you get to the overpass, it's just **a stone's throw**. It'll be **clear sailing** from there.
Driver:	OK. Thanks very much. So which would be the quickest way?
Attendant:	Oh, I'd say the back streets are **your safest bet**.
Driver:	OK thanks. I'd better **get a move on** if I want to make my appointments. I'll try the back streets and **keep my fingers crossed** that there're no more **hold ups**. Thanks again for your help.
Attendant:	Not a problem.

Now let's see what the underlined expressions mean - look at the next page.

CONVERSATION 2 (explanation of everyday expressions)

Compare Conversation 1 with Conversation 2 -**You will see that some of the words are different but the meaning is the same in both conversations. Find the underlined words in Conversation 1, then underline the words with the same meaning in Conversation 2.**
eg. I'm ***after*** some directions (Conversation 1) = I'm ***seeking/need*** some directions. (Conversation 2)

Attendant: Need some help?

Driver: Yeah, I'm <u>seeking/need</u> some directions. Could you tell me the best way to Fairgrove, please?

Attendant: Sure…now let me think which would be the best way to go this time of the day. You'll come to a crowded section of road if you go along the highway, so don't go that way.

Driver: I know/I agree. We've been in very slow moving traffic for the last hour on the highway. The traffic is in a queue to the first exit.

Attendant: Oh, well there's probably been an accident involving several cars again, if it's that bad.

Driver: Mm. And they've put in a lot of one way streets since I was last here and it's made me confused. I couldn't turn into a side road where I wanted to.

Attendant: Yeah, it's a bit difficult around here now but there're a couple of ways you can go other than the highway. You could avoid the city completely by taking the old road. I'll show you on the map there. See… see here.

Driver: Yes I see...on the other side of the highway.

Attendant: That's right. Be careful of the trucks on that road though… it winds quite a bit so it can get a bit dangerous; especially this time of day when the truck drivers are trying to avoid the traffic too.

Driver: OK. I'll remember that.

Attendant: Your other option is to go through the back streets. It is a shorter way but you won't avoid the traffic completely. Do a U-turn here (turn around and drive the opposite way) and then take the second on the right back there.

Driver: You mean back there, near the park?

Attendant: That's right. Turn right there. Go through two sets of lights. Take the next left and you'll come to a bend in the road. Follow that through, go over the overpass and you'll see signs to Fairgrove. Once you get to the overpass, it's just a short distance. It'll be easy from there.

Driver: OK. Thanks very much. So which would be the quickest way?

Attendant: Oh, I'd say the back streets are the best choice.

Driver: OK, thanks. I'd better hurry if I want to make my appointments. I'll try the backstreets and hope for good luck and success, that there are no more delays. Thanks again for your help.

Attendant: Not a problem.

Important note:
The language used in Conversation 2 (above) may seem easier to understand when compared with Conversation 1. However, the 'everyday' expressions used in Conversation 1 are used extensively by speakers of English. Therefore it is beneficial to become familiar with the everyday expressions used by the speakers in **Conversation 1.**

◀◀ **Replay Conversation 1**
Listen to the conversation again and fill in the missing words. You may have to listen more than once. (Don't worry about your spelling as this exercise focuses on listening skills - you can check your spelling later.)

Attendant:	Need some help?
Driver:	Yes, I'm **after** some directions. Could you tell me the best way to Fairgrove, please?
Attendant:	Sure...now let me think which'd be the best way to go this time of the day. You'll come to **a bottleneck** if you go along the highway, so don't go that way.
Driver:	_____ **me about it!** We've been in **bumper to** _____ **traffic** for the last hour on the highway. The traffic's **backed** _____ to the first exit.
Attendant:	Oh, well there's probably been a _____ **up** again if it's that bad.
Driver:	Mm. And they've put in a lot of one way streets since I was last here and it's completely **thrown me**. I couldn't **turn** _____ where I wanted to.
Attendant:	Yeah, it's a bit **tricky** around here now but there're a couple of ways you can go other than the highway. You could avoid the city completely by taking the old road. I'll show you on the map there. See…see here.
Driver:	Yes I see...on the other side of the highway.
Attendant:	That's right **Watch** _____ **for** trucks on that road though… it winds quite a bit so it can get a bit _____; especially this time of day when the truck drivers are trying to avoid the traffic too.
Driver:	OK. I'll _____ **that in mind**.
Attendant:	Your other option is to go through the backstreets. It is **a short** _____ but you won't avoid the traffic completely. Do a U-turn here and then take the second on the right back there.
Driver:	You mean back there, near the park?
Attendant:	That's right. Turn right there. Go through two sets of lights. Take the next left and you'll come to a bend in the road. Follow that through, go over the overpass and you'll see signs to Fairgrove. Once you get to the overpass, it's just **a stone's** _____. It'll be _____ **sailing** from there.
Driver:	OK. Thanks very much. So which would be the quickest way?
Attendant:	Oh, I'd say the back streets are **your safest** _____.
Driver:	OK thanks. I'd better _____ **a** _____ **on** if I want to make my appointments. I'll try the back streets and **keep my fingers** _____ that there're no more _____ **ups**. Thanks again for your help.
Attendant:	Not a problem.

Now check your answers by comparing this page with
CONVERSATION 1.

In order to become more familiar with these new everyday expressions:

◀◀ **Replay Conversation 1**

1) **Listen and tick the boxes** ☐ ✓ **next to the expressions as you hear them.**

2) **Write the definitions you can remember. (The first one has been done as an example.)**
   Check your answers with the reference list on page 125.

☐ after .... *seeking/looking for*

☐ a bottleneck............................ _____

☐ Tell me about it!............................ _____

☐ bumper to bumper traffic................ _____

☐ backed up .... _____

☐ a pile up..................................... _____

☐ thrown me..................................... _____

☐ turn off .... _____

☐ tricky... _____

☐ Watch out for.......................... _____

☐ hairy... _____

☐ keep (that) in mind .... _____

☐ a short cut...................................... _____

☐ a stone's thrown .... _____

☐ clear sailing........................... _____

☐ safest bet ….......................... _____

☐ get a move on ....…................ _____

☐ keep (my) fingers crossed.............. _____

☐ hold-ups .... _____

LANGUAGE NOTES:
'a bottleneck' refers to a crowded section of road where traffic can not pass easily, often caused by the road narrowing or resulting from an intersection of several roads .

'a hold-up' can refer to a situation that stops or delays something happening (for example, a delay on the highway as in Conversation 1 of this unit) or *'a hold-up'* can refer to an attempt to rob a place or person using a weapon.

Some people, when using the expression *'I'll keep my fingers crossed'*, actually cross their middle finger over their index finger to bring success or 'good luck'.

CROSSWORD – VOCABULARY REVISION

Complete the sentences, choosing from the everyday expressions which are listed below.
You can use the clues in brackets ( ) at the end of each sentence to help you.
Then complete the crossword using the everyday expressions you have written.
The first one has been done as an example. Answers, page 115.

a pile up	get a move on	turn off	clear sailing	~~a stone's throw~~	a short cut
bottleneck	hairy	bumper to bumper	tricky	fingers crossed	hold ups

ACROSS

1) The bank is just ***a stone's throw*** from my office. It's very convenient. (short distance)

3) Life can be _____ _____ if you have good health and a positive attitude. (easy)

5) The drive down the mountain is really _____It's steep and slippery. (dangerous/frightening)

7) I'm taking the train tomorrow. There were lots of _____ ___ on the highway today. (delays)

9) The traffic along the highway is usually _____ __ _____ every morning. (slow moving)

11) I'll keep my _____ _____ that you pass your driving test. (wish for luck/success)

DOWN

2) This game is a bit _____. (difficult)

4) Don't go that way! Go down the next road; it's __ _____ _____.(shorter way)

6) You'd better _____ ___ _____ ___ if you want to catch the ten o' clock train. (hurry)

8) There's been __ _____ ___ of ten cars on the highway. (road accident involving several cars)

10) You can't _____ ___ into that road any more. It's a one-way road now. (turn into a side road)

12) This area is a _____. They need to put in traffic lights. (crowded section of road)

			2								
1 a	*	s	t	o	n	e	'	s	*	t h r o w	

FOCUS ON SPOKEN LANGUAGE

A) Giving instructions or directions

When giving instructions or directions in English, we usually begin the instruction with a verb. Read the section below taken from Conversation 1 and notice the pattern used by the service station attendant when giving directions. The verbs are in *bold* at the beginning of each direction.

Notice the pattern used for giving directions. A verb begins each direction.

Verb	
Do	a U-turn here and then
take	the second on the right back there……….
Turn	right there.
Go	through two sets of lights.
Take	the next left and you'll come to a bend in the road.
Follow	that through,
go	over the overpass and you'll see signs to Fairgrove.

In grammar books, this pattern is called an *imperative*.
It is used when we want to be clear and direct with our information.

This pattern is also used for giving *instructions* on how to do or make something; for example, when giving instructions for games or recipes. The pattern is also used for giving *orders*, or when giving *warnings*. It may also used by parents or teachers to give *instructions*.

Look at the following imperatives. Match the imperative with the situation in which it would most likely be used. One has been done as an example. (Answers: page 115)

IMPERATIVE	SITUATION
Mix the sugar and milk together.	instruction for a game
Sit down and be quiet.	giving directions
Go up the stairs and then turn right.	a strong order
Be careful!	instruction for a recipe
Leave the building now!	instruction from parent to small child
Deal five cards to each player.	a warning regarding danger

In Conversation 1 (page 78), there are two other examples of imperatives in addition to the imperatives used by the service station attendant, to give directions.

One is a *warning* given by the attendant to the driver.
Check Conversation 1, and write the warning on the line below.

Attendant: _____

The other imperative is an *exclamation*, used by the driver to show strong agreement with the other speaker. This is a less usual way of using an imperative. Find an imperative in Conversation 1 (page 78) used to show strong agreement and write it on the line below.

Driver: _____

You can check your answers on page 115.

IMPORTANT CULTURAL NOTE:

As mentioned earlier, imperatives are used when we want to be direct when giving warnings, directions or instructions. However, you should not use this pattern when *requesting* service, assistance or information (from shop assistants, service people etc.) as it would be *too direct* and may cause offence.

For example, when ordering coffee at a restaurant you should *not* say, 'Give me coffee.'
You should say, *'Could I have* coffee, please.' or '*I'd like* coffee, please.' or '*I'll have* coffee, please. '

For practice with using polite language when requesting service, see *Understanding Spoken English, Book One, Unit 8, Part 6C.*

B) Incomplete sentences in spoken language

In conversational speech, speakers do not always use complete sentences. Words are often left out, if the meaning is clear without using a complete sentence. This aspect of language is referred to in language grammar books as '*ellipsis*'.

For example:	**Informal spoken language**	**Complete sentence**
	See you soon.	*I will* see you soon.
	Coming?	*Are you* coming?

Practice

The following incomplete sentences have been taken from Conversation 1. Words have been omitted from the beginning of each utterance. Write the complete sentence for each utterance on the lines provided below, then check your answers on page 115.

Informal spoken language	**Complete sentence**
Attendant: Need some help?	_____need some help?
Driver: You mean back there, near the park?	_____you mean back there, near the park?
Attendant: Not a problem.	_____not a problem.

C) Giving feedback - Showing you understand and checking information

When listening to instructions in English, it is very important to give 'feedback' to show that we understand what the speaker is saying. We do this by using such expressions as 'Yes,...', 'OK...', 'Sure', 'I see what you mean.....', etc.

It's also important to confirm or check that we have heard and understood the information correctly. We can do this by repeating the information or using expressions such as, 'Do you mean...'

How did the driver *confirm* that he understood the service station assistant's direction?
Check Conversation 1 (page 78) and complete the driver's reply on the line below.

Assistant:...I'll show you on the map there. See...see here.

Driver: _____

How did the driver *check* that he had understood the service station assistant's direction correctly?
Check Conversation 1 (page 78) and complete the driver's reply on the line below.

Attendant: Do a U-turn here and then take the second on the right back there.

Driver: _____

Attendant: That's right. Turn right there.

You can check your answers on page 115.

Feedback and conversational 'fillers'

In spoken English, we often begin a reply or comment with a word such as 'Well', 'Yes', 'OK', 'Mm', 'Oh'... etc. One reason for this is to show we are listening and interested in what is being said. These expressions also make speech more conversational; in fact a conversation without such expressions could sound rather abrupt and unfriendly.

◄◄ **Replay Conversation 1**
   Read and listen to Conversation 1 again and notice how many times these kinds of expressions are used throughout the conversation.

UNIT 8

FUTURE PLANS AND POSSIBILITIES

Do you plan for the future or do you just 'let things happen'? In this unit you will hear two friends, Chris and Kerri, talking about what they are going to do when they have finished their tourism course. Before you listen to the conversation, match the following words with the appropriate definition below. You can check your answers on page 116.

opportunity	ambitious	goal	voluntary (work)	experience

an aim for the future   _____   determined to be successful   _____

unpaid work   _____   skills learned from practice   _____

a useful situation, chance   _____

Now listen to the conversation and decide which of the following statements are true. (There may be more than one correct answer). You can check your answers on page 116.

1) Chris says he is going to:

     a) learn to fly.

     b) visit his family.

     c) look for a job.

2) Chris suggests that Kerri should:

     a) do some voluntary work.

     b) get a job in a shop.

     c) see a doctor.

3) Chris thinks:

     a) people have to plan if they want to succeed.

     b) it isn't important to plan for success.

4) Chris says he is:

     a) ambitious.

     b) lazy.

     c) rich.

Now, we'll look at the everyday expressions used in the conversation – turn to the next page.

CONVERSATION 1 (with everyday expressions)

◂◂ Replay Conversation 1
Read this conversation as you listen to the audio recording. Do you know what the
underlined **words mean? They are colloquial or 'everyday' expressions.**

Chris: Only one week left till the end of our course. I can't believe the year's **just about** over.

Kerri: Me neither.

Chris: What are you doing over the holiday period? Anything exciting?

Kerri: No, not really, Chris. I suppose, I'll just **play it by ear**. What about you? Any plans?

Chris: Yeah, I'm going to visit my family in the country for a week. I'm flying out next Wednesday. I haven't seen them for a while so I'm really **looking forward to** it. And then, when I come back, I'm going to look for a job...as a tour guide if possible.

Kerri: I guess, I'll look for a job too but I must say, I'm a bit **half hearted about** it.

Chris: Why's that?

Kerri: Well, **let's face it**, **every Tom, Dick and Harry** will be looking for work this time of year. And the other problem is, employers usually want experienced people, not students straight out of college.

Chris: True, so why not get some experience doing some voluntary work for a few weeks? That's what I'm going to do if I don't get a job **straight away.**

Kerri: Mm. I suppose it'd be better than sitting around, **twiddling my thumbs**. But I'm not really **taken with the idea** of working for nothing.

Chris: Well, the way I look at it, you'd be **killing two birds with one stone**. It'd be **paving the way** for future work and helping someone at the same time. And **you never know** - it may lead to a job later on.

Kerri: You know, I **have to hand it to you**, Chris. You seem to **have it all worked out**. I'm the sort of person who hopes opportunities'll **turn up** **out of the blue**. I don't plan ahead like you.

Chris: Well, **as far as I'm concerned**, you have to plan if you want be successful - if you just wait for something to turn up, it may never happen. I think we have to **set our sights on** what we want and then **go for it**! I suppose I'm ambitious but I believe we have to create our opportunities.

Kerri: Well, I can see you're going to **go places**, that's for sure. Maybe I should **get my act together** and set some goals too…Well, I'm going to get some lunch. How about you?

Chris: That sounds like a very good idea. I'll just let the others know...

Now let's see what the underlined expressions mean - look at the next page.

CONVERSATION 2 (explanation of everyday expressions)

Compare Conversation 1 with Conversation 2 -You will see that some of the words are different but the meaning is the same in both conversations. Find the underlined words in Conversation 1, then underline the words with the same meaning in Conversation 2. For example: *just about* (Conversation 1) = *almost* (Conversation 2)

Chris: (There is) only one week till the end of our course. I can't believe the year's <u>almost</u> over.

Kerri: Me neither.

Chris: What are you doing over the holiday period? Anything exciting?

Kerri: No, not really, Chris. I suppose, I'll just wait and see what happens (I don't have a plan). What about you? Any plans?

Chris: Yes, I'm going to visit my family in the country for a week. I'm flying out next Wednesday. I haven't seen them for a while so I'm really happily waiting for it. And then, when I come back, I'm going to look for a job…as a tour guide if possible.

Kerri: I guess I'll look for a job too but I must say, I'm a bit disinterested/only half interested in it.

Chris: Why's that?

Kerri: Well, we must accept the truth about this situation, a lot of ordinary people will be looking for work this time of year. And the other problem is, employers usually want experienced people, not students (who are) straight out of college.

Chris: True, so why not get some experience doing some voluntary work for a few weeks? That's what I'm going to do if I don't get a job immediately.

Kerri: Mm. I suppose it'd be better than sitting around being bored, doing nothing. But I'm not really happy about the idea of working for nothing.

Chris: Well, the way I look at it, you'd be achieving two things with one action. It'd be preparing the way for future work and helping someone at the same time. And there is a possibility-it may lead to a job later on.

Kerri: You know, I have to admire/congratulate you, Chris. You seem to have everything planned and organised. I'm the sort of person who hopes opportunities will arrive/happen unexpectedly (without planning). I don't plan ahead like you.

Chris: Well, in my opinion, you have to plan if you want be successful - if you just wait for something to turn up, it may never happen. I think we have to decide and aim for what we want and then try hard (to get what we want!) I suppose I'm ambitious but I believe we have to create our opportunities.

Kerri: Well, I can see you're going to be successful, that's for sure. Maybe I should get organised and set some goals too… Well, I'm going to get some lunch. How about you?

Chris: That sounds like a very good idea. I'll just let the others know…

Important note:
The language used in Conversation 2 (above) may seem easier to understand when compared with Conversation 1. However, the 'everyday' expressions used in Conversation 1 are used extensively by speakers of English. Therefore it is beneficial to become familiar with the everyday expressions used by the speakers in **Conversation 1**.

◄◄ **Replay Conversation 1**
Listen to the conversation again and fill in the missing words. You may need to listen more than once. (Don't worry about your spelling as this activity focuses on listening skills; you can check your spelling later.)

Chris: Only one week left till the end of our course. I can't believe the year's **just** _____ over.

Kerri: Me neither.

Chris: What are you doing over the holiday period? Anything exciting?

Kerri: No, not really Chris. I suppose, I'll just **play it by** _____. What about you? Any plans?

Chris: Yeah, I'm going to visit my family in the country for a week. I'm flying out next Wednesday. I haven't seen them for a while so I'm really **looking** _____ **to** it. And then, when I come back, I'm going to look for a job…. as a tour guide if possible.

Kerri: I guess, I'll look for a job too but I must say, I'm a bit _____ **hearted about** it.

Chris: Why's that?

Kerri: Well, **let's** _____ **it**, **every Tom, Dick and Harry** will be looking for work this time of year. And the other problem is, employers usually want experienced people, not students straight out of college.

Chris: True, so why not get some experience doing some voluntary work for a few weeks? That's what I'm going to do if I don't get a job _____ **away.**

Kerri: Mm. I suppose it'd be better than sitting around, **twiddling my** _____. But I'm not really _____ **with the idea** of working for nothing.

Chris: Well, the way I look at it, you'd be **killing two** _____ **with one stone**. It'd be **paving the way** for future work and helping someone at the same time. And **you never know** - it may lead to a job later.

Kerri: You know, I **have to** _____ **it to you**, Chris. You seem to **have it all worked** _____. I'm the sort of person who hopes opportunities'll **turn up out of the** _____. I don't plan ahead like you.

Chris: Well, **as** _____ **as I'm concerned**, you have to plan if you want be successful - if you just wait for something to turn up, it may never happen. I think we have to _____ **our sights on** what we want and then _____ **for it**! I suppose I'm ambitious but I believe we have to create our opportunities.

Kerri: Well, I can see you're going to **go** _____, that's for sure. Maybe I should _____ **my act together** and set some goals too…Well, I'm going to get some lunch. How about you?

Chris: That sounds like a very good idea. I'll just let the others know...

Now check your answers by comparing this page with Conversation 1.

In order to become more familiar with these new everyday expressions:

◀◀ **Replay Conversation 1**

1) **Listen and tick the boxes** ☑ **next to the expressions as you hear them.**

2) **Write the definitions you can remember. (The first one has been done as an example.)**
   Check your answers with the reference list on page 126.

☐ just about………………………..		almost
☐ play it by ear…………………….		
☐ looking forward to……………….		
☐ half hearted (about)………………		
☐ let's face it……………....……..		
☐ every Tom, Dick and Harry………..		
☐ straight away…………………….		
☐ twiddling my thumbs……………..		
☐ (not) taken with the idea………….		
☐ killing two birds with one stone…...		
☐ paving the way……………………		
☐ you never know…………………..		
☐ have to hand it to (you)…………....		
☐ have it all worked out…………….		
☐ turn up……………………………		
☐ out of the blue……………………..		
☐ as far as I'm concerned…………..		
☐ set (our) sights on ……………..…		
☐ go for it!…………………………..		
☐ go places………………………..…		
☐ get my act together……………….		

LANGUAGE NOTES:

The expression *'turn up'*, meaning 'arrive or happen', can be used for **people**, **events** and **things**.

For example: 'What time did Tom **turn up**?' = 'What time did Tom **arrive**?'

'Don't worry. Something will **turn up**.' = 'Something will **happen** to solve the problem.'

'Don't worry. Your purse will **turn up**.' = 'Your purse will **be found**.'

The expression, *'Let's face it'* is usually said before something that is **unpleasant** but true.

CROSSWORD - LANGUAGE REVISION

Complete the sentences, choosing from the expressions or words that are listed below.
You can use the clues in brackets ( ) at the end of each sentence to help you.
Then complete the crossword using the everyday expressions you have written.
The first one has been done as an example. Answers, page 116.

straight away	play it by ear	the blue	~~get my act together~~	you never know	face it
looking forward to	pave the way	just about	go places	half hearted	go for it

ACROSS

1) I should ***get my act together*** and start saving to buy a house. (get organised)

3) We haven't planned anything for Sunday. We'll just _____ ___ ___ _____. (see what happens)

5) This course will _____ _____ _____ for the job I really want. (prepare the way)

7) Let's _____ _____. Our business isn't doing well. (accept the truth about this situation)

9) When he got the message, he rang them _____ _____. (immediately)

11) I'm _____ _____ about my new job. I don't really like it. (not very interested)

13) I think you should go to the dance tonight. _____ _____ _____ - you may meet your perfect partner. (there is a possibility)

DOWN

2) If you really want to be an actor, then I think you should ____ _____ ___. (try hard to succeed)

4) We are _____ _____ ___ seeing their new baby. (happily awaiting)

6) He is going to ____ _____. Look how well he is progressing already. (be successful)

8) I have _____ _____ finished painting the house. (almost)

10) He was very healthy until suddenly, out of _____ _____, he became sick. (unexpectedly)

Answers, page 116.

FOCUS ON SPOKEN LANGUAGE - Talking about the future

There are several verb forms used to talk about the future in English.

- We talk about our **plans and intentions** - this will be examined in section **A** and **B**.
- We **predict what we think will happen** - this will be examined in section **C**.
- We talk about **definite future arrangements** - this will be examined in section **D**.

In section **A** and **B** we examine two verb forms which were used by the speakers in Conversation 1 to talk about their **plans and intentions**.

- **will** + verb   eg. I'**ll** just **play** it by ear. (I **will** is usually contracted to I **'ll**).
- **am going to** +verb   eg. I'**m going to visit** my family in the country for a week.

A) Talking about future plans and intentions

We use **will** when we are deciding at the moment of speaking what we will do.
For this reason, **I'll** is often used with expressions such as '**I think**', '**I suppose**', or '**I guess**'.
The following sentences have been taken from Conversation 1. In each example, the speaker is **making a decision at the time of speaking**.

Exercise 1

Find the sentences in Conversation 1 (page 88), then complete each utterance with **will** + **verb**.

Kerri: I suppose, I_____just _____ it by ear.

Kerri: I guess, I_____ for a job too…

Chris: I_____just _____the others know…   Answers, page 116.

In each of the above sentences, the speakers are making a decision at the moment of speaking. They had not decided or planned their action before speaking.

Notice the pattern: will   +   verb (base form)

I suppose	I'**ll** (just)	**play** it by ear.
I guess	I'**ll**	**look** for a job too…
	I'**ll** (just)	**let** the others know…

Exercise 2

Complete the following conversations. Remember, the second speakers are making their decision at **the moment of speaking**, so use **will** + **verb**. Answers, page 116.

1st Speaker: This is so heavy!

2nd Speaker: Wait a minute. I _____you.

1st Speaker: Oh, I forgot to post these letters!

2nd Speaker: Don't worry. I _____them later.

B) Talking about pre-planned decisions

We use *going to* when we talk about things that *have been decided or planned <u>before</u> the moment of speaking*. The following sentences have been taken from Conversation 1 (page 88). In each example, the speaker had made their decision *before* the time of speaking. Find the sentences in Conversation 1 (page 88), and complete each sentence with *am + going to + verb*.

am + going to + verb (base form)   Answers, page 116.

Yes, I'***m***	*going to*	*visit* my family in the country for a week.
...... I'***m***		for a job.......as a tour guide if possible.
That's what I'***m***		if I don't get a job straight away.
Well, I'		some lunch.

Note: Because *going to + verb* suggests *premeditated intention*, it is **not** usually used with expressions such as, *'I think', 'I guess'* or *'I suppose'* when talking about plans. For example, we would **not** say, *'I think* I'm going to get some lunch.

Remember * We use *will* when the speaker decides/plans *at the time of speaking*.
         * We use *going to* when the decision was made *before* the time of speaking.

Practice

Complete the following conversation about future plans using *will* or *going to.*

Sue: What are you <u>going to</u> do on Saturday?

Pat: I'm not sure yet. I think I_____ stay home and study.

Sue: Jenni and I are _____ go to the beach. Would you like to come?

Pat: Yes. That sounds great! I _____ study on Sunday instead.

Sue: OK. We're _____ catch the bus at 8 a.m.

Pat: OK. I _____ meet you at the bus stop then. What are you _____ take for lunch?

Sue: I'm not sure yet. I guess I _____ just take some fruit and some sandwiches.

(Answers: page 116)

C) Making Predictions

When we predict (say what we think will happen in the future), we can use *will or going to.*
For example: 'It'*s going to rain* tomorrow.'   or 'I think, it *will rain* tomorrow.'
'I'*m going to have* a big phone bill this month.'   or   'I'*ll have* a big phone bill this month.'

In Conversation 1, Kerri makes a prediction about Chris.
Read Conversation 1 again, find and complete the following sentence.

Kerri: ......I can see_____ *go places.*   Answers, page 116.

• Make a prediction about your next telephone bill. How much do you think it will be?

*My next phone bill*_____

• Make a prediction about the weather tomorrow.

*Tomorrow*_____

D) Talking about definite future arrangements

When we talk about *definite plans that have already been arranged*, we often use the present progressive tense (also called the present continuous tense). The *present progressive tense* is formed with *am, are,* or *is* + *ing*. We use it to talk about plans that are definite.

Practice

Refer to Conversation 1 (page 88, line 5) and complete the following sentence.

Chris: 'Yes, I'm going to visit my family in the country for a week. I _____ out next Wednesday.'

Chris uses the *present progressive tense (am flying)* because the plan is definite.
It is about a *present*, as well as *future* situation - he already has his airline ticket.

Look at the following conversation about future plans and happenings.

Lin: 'What *are* you *doing* at the end of the year?
    Are you *going* away for a vacation?'

Ann: 'Not this year. I*'m having** a baby in January,
    so *we're staying* at home in December.'

Ann used the *present progressive tense* (*am having*)
because there is *present* evidence of her baby's future birth.
In the same situation, Ann may also say, 'I'm *going to have*
a baby in January, so we're *going to stay* at home this Christmas.'

Note: Native speakers do **not** usually say,
'I*'ll* have a baby in January, so we*'ll* stay at home in December'

> *The verb *'have'* is used in a variety of ways in English. See Unit 9, Part 6B for details.

Practice

Do you have any definite arrangements for next week? (eg. appointments, visits, classes?)
Complete the following sentence with information about you, using *am* + ...*ing*...

Next week, I'm_____.

Revision and Practice - Talking about the future
Complete the following conversation by writing the correct verb in the spaces.

Use *will, am/is going to,* or *am/is ...ing* (present progressive tense) with the verb in brackets.
The first one has been done as an example. You can check your answers on page 117.

Rai: What **are** you **going to do** (do) while you're on holidays next week?

Jan: I_____(stay) with my sister, Kate, and help her look after her two small sons.

Rai: Why? Is she sick?

Jan: No. She_____(have) another baby.

Rai: Really? In that case, I_____(call) her on the phone tonight and congratulate her.

Jan: Oh good! I'm sure, she_____(be) happy to hear from you.

Rai: In fact, I think I_____(go) to the shops tomorrow and buy a
    present for her. Any ideas?

Jan: Well, the weather_____(be) hot when the baby's born...

Rai: I know! I_____(buy) her a fan!

UNIT 9

HAVING DINNER WITH FRIENDS

Listening for general understanding

In this Unit you will listen to a conversation between friends, Mal, Lee and Julie, who are having dinner together at a restaurant. The conversation contains 'everyday' expressions that will be explained later in the unit - so don't worry if you don't understand every word. This time you are only listening for a general understanding of the topic.

As you listen again, tick the correct answers below. (There may be more than one correct answer.) When you have finished you can check your answers on page 117.

1) Which of the following meals do you hear mentioned?

        a) roast beef

        b) salad

        c) vegetable loaf

        d) fish with chill sauce

2) How many of the friends are going to order fish?

        a) none

        b) one

        c) two

        d) three

3) What kind of movie did Lee and Mal see last night?

        a) a comedy (funny movie)

        b) an adventure movie

        c) a sad movie

Now, we'll look at the everyday expressions used in the conversation – turn to the next page.

CONVERSATION 1 (with everyday expressions)

◀◀ **Replay Conversation 1**
Read this conversation as you listen to the audio recording. Do you know what the _underlined_ words mean? They are colloquial or 'everyday' expressions.

Mal: Well, I know what I'm going to have…What about you two?

Lee: Mm. It's **a toss up** between the roast beef and the vegetable loaf. What've you decided on?

Mal: I'm going to have the fish with chilli sauce. It was delicious last time.

Lee: Mm…I love seafood too but spicy food **doesn't agree with me**; so I won't have that.

Julie: Me neither. I'm going to **steer clear of** fish from now on. I had some that was **off** a few months ago and I **can't stand** it now.

Lee: Really? You didn't have it here, did you?

Julie: No, no. It was at the seafood restaurant on North Street. When I told them about it they offered me a meal **on the house** but I haven't been back since.

Lee: Well, **I don't blame you**. I heard that place isn't much good anyway. Now, what'll I have... I think, I'll **go for** the vegetable loaf.

Julie: Me too. The vegetarian food's always good here. And what about something to drink? Would you like some wine?

Lee: Mm. That sounds like a good idea.

Mal: Not for me thanks…but the drinks are **on me** this time. You paid for the last **round**.

Julie: Oh OK, thanks Mal. Would you like a bottle of red or white, Lee?

Lee: **I'm easy**, you decide…Oh, **on second thoughts**, maybe we should buy it by the glass. We're having an important meeting at work tomorrow, so I don't want to have **a hangover**.

Julie: That's OK. Don't worry. I'll **polish off** what you can't drink… So tell me about the movie you went to see last night.

Mal: Oh I thought it was **a scream**. It was a comedy about marriage and I was **in stitches**. You weren't really **taken with** it though were you, Lee?

Lee: Oh it was OK. It was a bit **over the top**, that's all - a bit **far-fetched**, you know.

Mal: Yeah but that's what made it so funny.

Julie: Well it looks like I'll have to go and **check it out** myself.

Mal: Here comes the waiter. What're we all having again?

Now let's see what the underlined expressions mean - look at the next page.

CONVERSATION 2 (explanation of everyday expressions)

Compare Conversation 1 with Conversation 2 -You will see that some of the words are different but the meaning is the same in both conversations. Find the underlined words in Conversation 1, then underline the words with the same meaning in Conversation 2. For example: <u>a toss up</u> (Conversation 1) = <u>an equal choice/decision</u> (Conversation 2)

Mal: Well, I know what I'm going to have....What about you two?

Lee: It's <u>an equal choice/decision</u> between the roast beef and the vegetable loaf. What've you decided on?

Mal: I'm going to have the fish with chilli sauce. It was delicious last time.

Lee: Mm...I love seafood too but spicy food isn't good for my health; so I won't have that.

Julie: Me neither. I'm going to avoid fish from now on. I had some that was bad/stale a few months ago and I dislike it (very much) now.

Lee: Really? You didn't have it here, did you?

Julie: No, no. It was at the seafood restaurant on North Street. When I told them about it, they offered me a meal at no cost/ free (at the management's expense) but I haven't been back since.

Lee: Well, I understand your decision. I heard that place isn't much good, anyway. Now, what'll I have...I think, I'll choose/have the vegetable loaf.

Julie: Me too. The vegetarian food is always good here. And what about something to drink? Would you like some wine?

Lee: Mm. That sounds like a good idea.

Mal: Not for me thanks...but the drinks are my expense (I'll pay for you) this time. You paid for the last set of drinks, one for each person.

Julie: Oh OK, thanks Mal. Would you like a bottle of red or white, Lee?

Lee: I'm happy with either choice, you decide...Oh, after thinking more about it, maybe we should buy it by the glass. We're having an important meeting at work tomorrow, so I don't want a headache etc. caused by too much alcohol.

Julie: That's OK. Don't worry. I'll finish what you can't drink... So tell me about the movie you went to see last night.

Mal: Oh I thought it was a very funny (thing). It was a comedy about marriage and I was laughing very much. You weren't really impressed with it though were you, Lee?

Lee: Oh it was OK. It was a bit exaggerated /extreme, that's all - a bit unbelievable (difficult to believe the story was possible), you know.

Mal: Yes but that's what made it so funny.

Julie: Well it looks like I'll have to go and see/investigate it myself.

Mal: Here comes the waiter. What're we all having again?

Important note:
The language used in Conversation 2 (above) may seem easier to understand when compared with Conversation 1. However, the 'everyday' expressions used in Conversation 1 are used extensively by speakers of English. Therefore it is beneficial to become familiar with the everyday expressions used by the speakers in **Conversation 1**.

◄◄ Replay Conversation 1
Listen to the conversation again and fill in the missing words. You may have to listen more than once. (Don't worry about your spelling as this exercise focuses on listening skills - you can check your spelling later.)

Mal: Well, I know what I'm going to have….What about you two?

Lee: It's **a toss** ___ between the roast beef and the vegetable loaf. What've you decided on?

Mal: I'm going to have the fish with chilli sauce. It was delicious last time.

Lee: Mm…I love seafood too but spicy food **doesn't** ___ **with me**; so I won't have that.

Julie: Me neither. I'm going to **steer** ___ of fish from now on. I had some that was **off** a few

months ago and I **can't** ___ it now.

Lee: Really? You didn't have it here, did you?

Julie: No, no. It was at the seafood restaurant on North Street. When I told them about it they

offered me a meal **on the** ___ but I haven't been back since.

Lee: Well, **I don't blame you**. I heard that place isn't much good anyway. Now, what'll I have…

I think, I'll ___ **for** the vegetable loaf.

Julie: Me too. The vegetarian food's always good here. And what about something to drink?

Would you like some wine?

Lee: Mm. That sounds like a good idea.

Mal: Not for me thanks…but the drinks are ___ **me** this time. You paid for the last ___.

Julie: Oh OK, thanks Mal. Would you like a bottle of red or white, Lee?

Lee: **I'm** ___, you decide…Oh, **on** ___ **thoughts**, maybe we should buy it by the glass.

We're having an important meeting at work tomorrow, so I don't want to have **a hangover**.

Julie: That's OK. Don't worry. I'll **polish** ___ what you can't drink…So tell me about the movie

you went to see last night.

Mal: Oh I thought it was **a** ___. It was a comedy about marriage and I was **in stitches**.

You weren't really **taken with** it though were you, Lee?

Lee: Oh it was OK. It was a bit **over the** ___, that's all. A bit ___ **-fetched**, you know.

Mal: Yes but that's what made it so funny.

Julie: Well it looks like I'll have to go and **check it** ___ myself.

Mal: Here comes the waiter. What're we all having again?

Now check your answers by comparing this page with Conversation 1.

In order to become more familiar with these new everyday expressions:

◀◀ **Replay Conversation 1**

1) **Listen and tick the boxes ☒ next to the expressions as you hear them.**
2) **Write the definitions you can remember. (The first one has been done as an example.)**
   Check your answers with the reference list on page 127.

☐ a toss up.. _an equal choice between two things_

☐ doesn't agree with me................... _____

☐ steer clear of............................... _____

☐ off.. _____

☐ can't stand.................................... _____

☐ on the house................................. _____

☐ I don't blame you.......................... _____

☐ go for.. _____

☐ (the drinks) are on me .... _____

☐ round (of drinks)........................... _____

☐ I'm easy.. _____

☐ on second thoughts....................... _____

☐ a hangover.................................... _____

☐ polish off...................................... _____

☐ a scream...................................... _____

☐ in stitches.................................... _____

☐ taken with................................... _____

☐ over the top .... _____

☐ far-fetched................................... _____

☐ check it out.................................. _____

CULTURAL NOTE:

When refusing food that has been offered to you, it may be offensive to refuse by saying: 'I don't like it'. However, to say '*It doesn't agree with me*', (meaning the food 'will have a bad reaction on my health') should not cause offence as it is a health issue rather than a rejection of the food. For example, I may like milk but be unable to eat food containing milk because it '*doesn't agree with*' my health.

CROSSWORD - LANGUAGE REVISION

Complete the sentences, choosing from the everyday expressions that are listed below.
You can use the clues in brackets ( ) at the end of each sentence to help you.
Then complete the crossword using the everyday expressions you have written.
One has been done as an example. Answers, page 117.

---

off   steer clear of   taken with   far-fetched   over the top   polished off

hangover   a scream   toss up   ~~on second thoughts~~   on the house

---

ACROSS

1) I'll finish my essay today…..***on second thoughts***, I won't have time to finish it till tomorrow. (after thinking about it some more)

3) I'm going to _____ _____ ___ the new car park. It's always too busy. (avoid)

5) The story he told us was too_____ _____. I didn't believe a word of it. (unbelievable)

7) It's opening night at our new restaurant so to celebrate, the drinks are ___ _____ _____. (free)

9) I don't think you should cook that fish. It smells _____. (bad/ stale)

11) I don't know which hat to buy. It's a _____ ____between the red or green one. (an equal choice)

DOWN

2) We've heard that the show is ___ _____ so we've booked seats to see it. (very funny)

4) I think the costumes in the parade were _____ _____ _____.(exaggerated/too extreme)

6) Who _____ _____ all the cake? There's none left! (finished)

8) If you drink more beer, you'll have a _____tomorrow. (headache from too much alcohol)

10) She's very _____ _____her new teacher. She thinks he's very clever. (impressed by)

Answers, page 117.

FOCUS ON SPOKEN LANGUAGE
A) Using 'too'/'neither' to agree with another person's choice, opinion or decision

1) Me neither

Note: *neither* can be pronounced as /niːðə/ (like the word kn<u>ee</u>) or /naɪðə/ (like the word n<u>igh</u>t).

In Conversation 1, Julie agreed with Lee's decision *not* to order fish for dinner. Read Conversation 1 again (page 98), and note the expression she used to agree with Lee's choice *not* to have seafood. Complete the conversation by writing the expression that Julie used in the space below.

> Lee: Mm...I love seafood too but spicy food doesn't agree with me. So I *won't* have that.
> Julie: _____. I'm going to steer clear of fish from now on. I had some that was off a few months ago and I can't stand it now.
>
> Answer, page 117.

When used in this way, '*neither*' means '*also not*'.
In spoken language we can use, '*Me neither*', when we want to *agree with a <u>negative</u> statement*.
For example, 'I ca*n't* speak French.' - 'Me *neither*'. This means, 'I *also can <u>not</u>* speak French.'
('*Neither can I*' and '*Nor can I*' have the same meaning).

Look at the following examples:

Lee's choice/opinion	Julie thinks the same as Lee.	Mal thinks differently to Lee.
I *won't* have fish.	Me *neither*. (also *Neither will I*.)	I will (have fish).
I*'m not* going to have wine.	Me *neither*. (also *Neither am I*.)	I am (going to have wine).
I *didn't* like the movie.	Me *neither*. (also *Neither did I*.)	I did (enjoy the movie).

2) Me too
Later in the conversation, Julie *agreed* with Lee's decision about having vegetable loaf for dinner. What did she say? Check Conversation 1 (page 98) and fill in the missing expression.

> Lee: Now what'll I have.....I think, I'*ll* go for the vegetable loaf.
> Julie: _____. The vegetarian food's always good here.

In spoken language we use, '*Me too*', when we want to *agree with a <u>positive</u> statement*.
For example, 'I'*m* studying English'. - 'Me *too*.' (This means: I *am also* studying English.)
('*So am I*.' has the same meaning).

Practice

3) Look at the following conversation about food preferences.
Fill in the missing words, using *too* and *neither*.

Bev: I *don't* eat dairy products much these days. They don't agree with me.
Noni: Me _____. I'm allergic to milk.
Bev: I *can't* stand cheese.
Noni: Me_____ . It makes me feel sick.
Bev: And I *don't* like yogurt.
Noni: Oh, I do. I think it's really nice. I have it sometimes with fruit and nuts.
Bev: But I love ice cream, of course, even though it's a dairy product.
Noni: Me _____. It's delicious!

B) Uses of the word 'have'

The verb *'have'* is used in a variety of ways in English.
Look at these examples from Conversation 1 of this Unit.

> I know what I'm going to *have*…
> You didn't *have* it here, did you?
> We're *having* an important meeting at work tomorrow.
> It looks like I'll *have* to go and check it out myself.

As an ordinary verb, *'have'* can refer to a variety of different activities. For example:

- *'have'* can mean 'produce, give birth to' eg. She's going to *have* a baby in March.

- *'have'* can mean 'engage in an activity'. eg. *have* a conversation; *have* a bath; *have* a party.

- *'have'* can mean 'undergo an experience'. eg. *have* an operation; *have* a good time.

- *'have'* can mean 'be part of a relationship'. eg. I *have* two brothers. I *have* a large family.

- *'have'* can mean 'possess a characteristic' eg I *have* black hair. They *have* poor eyesight.

- *'have'* can mean 'partake of food or drink'. eg. Let's *have* dinner. I'm going to *have* a drink.

- *'have'* can mean 'use/take' eg. *'Have* a seat, please. The doctor will see you soon.'

- *'have'* can mean 'employ someone to do' eg. I *have* my windows cleaned every month.

- *'have'* can mean 'to own/ possess' eg. I *have* a driver's licence. I *have* a cat. I *have* a business.

    In British English, *'have got'* is often used. eg. I *'ve got* a problem. *Have* you *got* a new car?

    In other English speaking countries, notably America, *do* is used with *have* in questions and negatives. eg *Do* you *have* a problem? I *don't have* time. (Rather than 'I *haven't got* time.')

    Note: When the meaning is 'to own/ possess', there is no difference in meaning between,
    Do you *have* a car?/*Have* you *got* a car?
    I *have* a car./I *'ve got* a car.
    I *don't have* a car. /I *haven't got* a car.

Other uses of *'have'*:

- *'have to'* + verb expresses obligation (similar meaning to *must*) eg. I *have to go* to class now. (Also: I *'ve got to go* to class now).

- *have* serves as an auxiliary (helper verb) in the present perfect tense.
    eg. I*'ve written* a letter; I *haven't finished*; *Have* you *seen* the movie, 'Star Wars'?

Reference Page
Countable and Uncountable nouns (also called **mass** or **non-count** nouns)

English nouns can be divided into countable and uncountable nouns.
Countable nouns can be counted and made plural. For example: cup<u>s</u>, table<u>s</u>, knive<u>s</u>.

An uncountable noun is one that has no plural form; it is considered as a 'mass'.
Some commonly used uncountable nouns are:

Names of substances, such as:

**water, ice, gas, fuel, petrol, oil, grease, milk, cream, tea, coffee, beer, wine,
soap, cloth, stone, gold, sand, glass, wood, dust, air, hair**

Names of abstract nouns (things we can experience but not always see), such as:

fear, courage, love, death, hope, advice, knowledge, work, time,

Names of categories, such as:

equipment, furniture, luggage, rubbish, shopping, money, information

Note that some words in the lists above, when used in a particular way, can be 'counted'.
For example: People say, 'I'll have three coffees, please', meaning 'three <u>cups</u> of coffee'.

Individual items within a category may be counted even though the category is uncountable.
For example, 'equipment' is uncountable but a group of individual 'tools' (which add up
to make the 'equipment' can be counted.

uncountable
eg. People say, We'll have to take a lot of equipment'

or

'We'll have to take a lot of tool<u>s</u> and thing<u>s</u>.' (the tools and things can be counted)
countable

Uncountable nouns are preceded by the following expressions which indicate the amount.

Quantifiers to indicate 'some' or 'more'		Quantifiers to indicate 'less' or 'none'	
some	quite a bit of	not much	not (have) any
a lot of	a large amount of	very little	no + noun
a great deal of		only a bit of	

Note: Some words which are considered 'uncountable' in English are countable in other languages.
For example, hair, information, rubbish, furniture, luggage are countable in some languages.

(Units 7 - 9)

This section reviews some of the expressions which were introduced in Units 7, 8, and 9 and gives you a chance to see what you have remembered.

- Look at the pictures on the opposite page and decide what the people are saying by choosing from the expressions below.

- Match each picture with an appropriate expression by writing the correct letter in the box next to each expression.

- For extra practice, you could write the appropriate expression in the space provided in the picture.

1) 'Who polished off all the ice cream?' ☐

2) 'We'll be in bumper to bumper traffic for hours because of this hold up.' ☐

3) 'This looks like fun! Let's make the most of it!' ☐

4) 'There's been a few piles ups along this road. The cars go too fast!' ☐

5) 'That ride was a bit hairy. I won't try that again!' ☐

6) 'This round's on me.' ☐

7) 'No thankyou. It looks delicious but seafood doesn't agree with me.' ☐

8) 'It'll be clear sailing if you make time to study each day.' ☐

9) 'I can't stand these 'Do it Yourself' projects;
    I'll cross my fingers that it all fits together.' ☐

Answers: page 118

ANSWERS TO UNIT ONE - A TELEPHONE ENQUIRY

Part 1

1) b) an Office Skills Course
2) c) three weeks ago
3) a) it's too late to start
   b) the class is full

4) b) 15th
5) b) Lea

Part 5 - Crossword

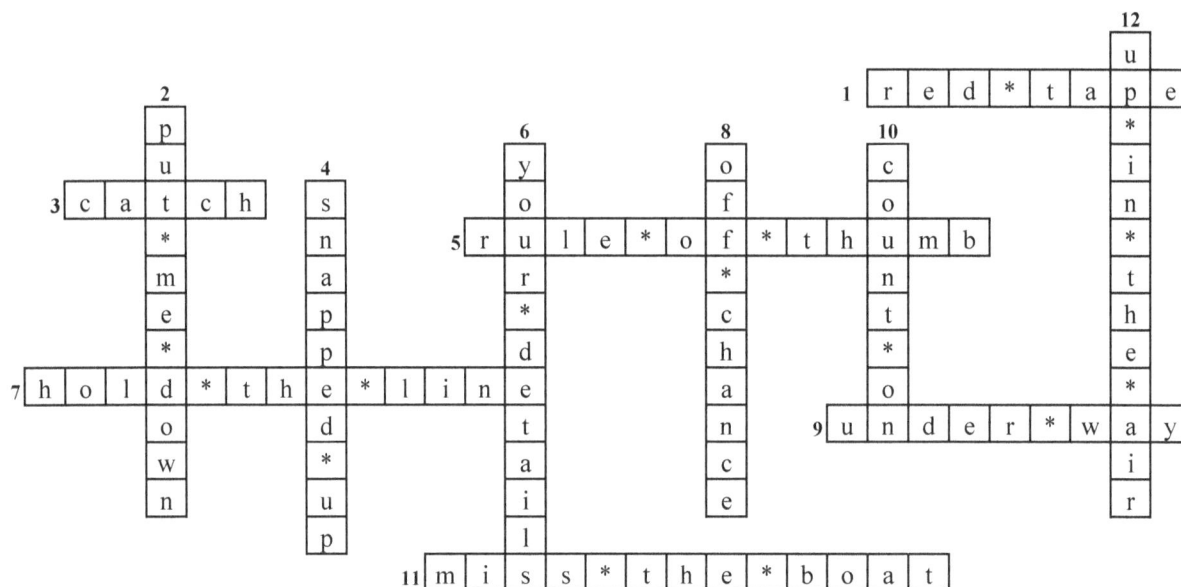

Across:
1 red * tape
3 catch
5 rule * of * thumb
7 hold * the * line
9 under * way
11 miss * the * boat

Down (letters shown in grid):
- 2: p u * m e * d o w n
- 4: s n a p p e d * u p
- 6: y o r * d e t a i l
- 8: o f * c h a n c e
- 10: c o n t * o
- 12: u p * i n * t h e * a i r

Part 6   Focus on Spoken Language

A) Checking information such as correct place/number
Chris: <u>Yes. Is that the business college</u>?

B) Giving a Reason for the Phone Call
Note, below is an example answer, however, variations of this are possible.

Receptionist:	West Town College. Can I help you?
You:	Yes. <u>Is that the English language college</u>?
Receptionist:	Yes. That's right.
You:	I'd like to <u>speak to someone about joining the English class that was advertised in the local paper</u>, please.
Receptionist:	Hold the line please. I'll put you through.
Assistant:	Good afternoon, English department. Can I help you?
You:	Yes. I'd like <u>to join the English class</u>, please.

C) Noticing 'weak forms' in spoken English

Chris:	I'd like *to* speak *to* someone about joining the Office Skills course please.
Receptionist:	Hold *the* line, please. I'll put you through.

Part 1

1) c)   her teacher is not pleased with her assignment;
   d)   she may fail her course
2) b)   leave/quit college
3) a)   transfer to a different course.
   c)   ask the teacher how she can improve her assignment

Part 5 - Crossword

```
                                                              2
                                                              g
                               4                6             e
                               c                t             t
                  8            a                h             *
        1  n o t * u p * t o * p a r             r             t
                  u            c                o             h
                  r            h       3 n o t * c u t * o u t * f o r
                  n            *                w             u        10
        5  k e e p * u p       u       3                      g         k
                  u            p                i             h         n
        7  g i v e * u p                        n                       u
                                                *                       c
                 12                             t       9 p i e c e * o f * c a k e
                  p                             h                       l
                  o                             *                       e
                  i                             t                       *
        11 g e t * s t u c k * i n t o * i t    o                       d
                  e                             w                       o
                  r                             e                       w
                  s                             l                       n
```

Part 6   Focus on Spoken Language

A)   Making Suggestions

1) 'Well <u>maybe you could</u> transfer to a course more suited to you'.
2) 'Well in that case, <u>why don't you</u> go and talk to your teacher'?

Most direct	1	Go and talk to your teacher.
	2	You should go and talk to your teacher.
	3	Why don't you go and talk to your teacher?
Least direct	4	Well, maybe you could go and talk to your teacher.

B)   Giving Reasons

No. I don't stand a chance of getting into another course now – it's too late. ***Besides***, I'd prefer to see this course through if I'm going to do anything.

Part 1

skills and talents (things you can do)	*abilities*
summary of education and work experience	*résumé (also CV)*
emergency medical treatment	*first aid*
training and educational accomplishments	*qualifications*
the work of keeping things in good condition	*maintenance*
manager	*supervisor*
related to the subject receiving attention	*relevant*
a person who does household repairs	*handyman*

1) a) he's just returned from a working holiday
2) b) a maintenance worker
   c) an office worker
3) a) a current driver's licence
   b) first aid certificate
4) a) improve his resume
   c) write a letter of application

Part - 5   Crossword

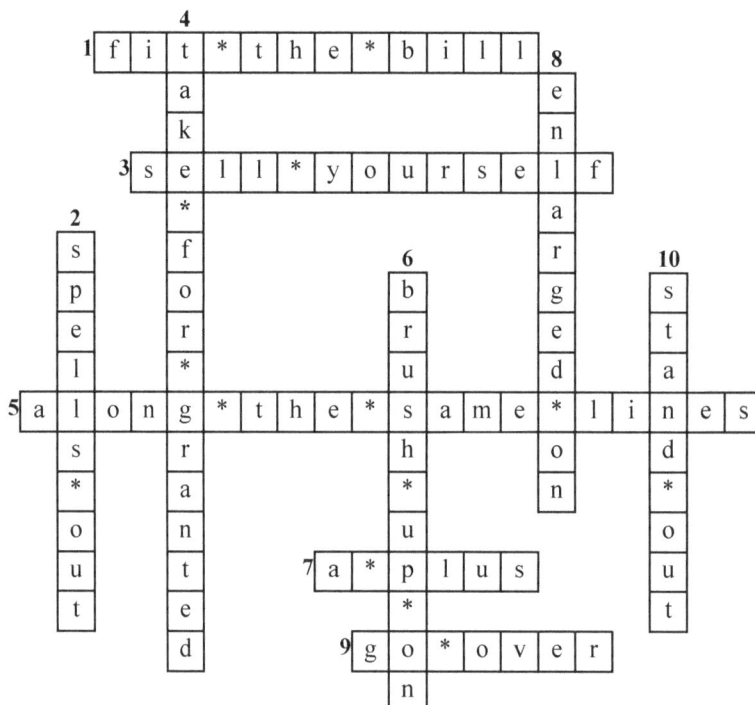

Across: 1 fit the bill; 3 sell yourself; 5 along the same lines; 7 a plus; 9 go over

Down: 2 spell out; 4 take five; 6 brush up; 8 enlarge; 10 standout

Part 6   Focus on Spoken Language

C) Talking about the Past (using present perfect and simple past tenses) Practice Answers

Some possible verbs are:

Have you *completed* your training yet?	Yes, I *finished/completed* my course in 2003.
Have you *used* this computer program before?	No, I *used* another program in my last job.
Have you *worked* in a shoe factory before?	Yes, I *worked* in a big shoe factory in Taiwan.
Have you *operated* this type of machine before?	Yes, I *operated/used* one like this in my last job.

D) 'Yes, I was away for about a year on a working holiday. I had a variety of different jobs.'

1) E		4) H		7) C	
2) F		5) G		8) D	
3) B		6) I		9) A	

ANSWERS TO UNIT FOUR - TECHNOLOGY AND BUSINESS

Part 1

a person controlled by someone/something - **slave**	change to a new system - **changeover**
a branch of production/manufacture - **industry**	expensive/ costing a lot of money - **costly**

1) b)	business is not going well	3)	a)	invest in some better technology
2) b)	the printing industry	4)	b)	thinks things are changing too quickly

Part 5   Crossword

Part 6   Focus on Spoken Language
A) Listening Practice

Manager: Oh Kim! Do you have a **minute**? I'd like to **discuss** a few things with you.... As you know, **sales** have been falling off over the past few **months**...and **between** you and me, things **aren't** looking very **good**.

Assistant: Well.....

Manager: Look, **before** you say **anything**, I'm not pointing the **finger** at you. I know you've suggested **several** times that we need to go in for better **equipment** if we're going to hold our own in the **industry**. And I have to go **along** with you now. It's time to bite the bullet and **invest** in some better **technology**.

Dictionary Practice:

discus (noun) *round, flat object thrown in sports events*	discuss (verb) *to talk about something*
rebel (noun) *a person who does not obey authority*	rebel (verb) *to refuse to obey*
present (noun) 1. *a gift* 2. *now (here now)*	present (verb) *to give or offer something*
object (noun) *a thing that can be seen and touched*	object (verb) *to complain or oppose to something*

B) Using adjectives ending with 'ed' or 'ing'

1)

1a) She was amaz**ed** by the story.	1b) She thought the story was amaz**ing**.
2a) I feel relax**ed** at the beach.	2b) The beach is relax**ing**.
3a) I get bor**ed** at school.	3b) I think school is **boring.**
4a) I get **tired** when I study for too long.	4b) It's tir**ing** to study for too long.
5a) I was **frightened** by the movie.	5b) The movie was frighten**ing**.
6a) I get excit**ed** when I watch soccer.	6b) I think soccer is an **exciting** game.
7a) I am annoy**ed** by her letter.	7b) Her letter is **annoying**.

2)

The sports competition was very **exciting**. Everyone in the audience was cheering and clapping. We were all very **excited** when the winner was announced. I was **amazed** to see how fast the competitors could run. Their speeds were **amazing**.

Unfortunately, the speeches that followed the competition were a bit **boring**. I usually get **bored** when people keep talking for a long time. In fact, I started to feel so **tired** I had trouble keeping my eyes open. It had been a very **interesting** but **tiring** day.

C) Discourse Markers

Assistant:…So when do you think we'll start the changeover?
Manager: The sooner the better**,** *I suppose*. There're some big changes to make and I'm not really looking forward to them. You know …. *I wonder* whether all this new technology is really making our lives easier. *It seems* to me we've created a vicious circle......
Assistant: What do you mean?
Manager: Well, technology's supposed to have given us more time and freedom but *it seems* we're becoming slaves to technology…

ANSWERS TO UNIT FIVE - A NEW VENTURE - MAKING DECISIONS

Part   1

1) b)   a coffee shop.

2) b)   High Street

3) a)   special introductory prices; b) an 'Under New Management' sign.

4) c)   write a list of the pros and cons.

Part 5   Crossword

Across:
1. come across
3. take the plunge
5. get your fingers burned
7. weigh up
9. toying with the idea
11. through the grapevine

Down:
2. pros and cons
4. looking into
6. off the ground
8. going for a song
10. up and running
12. elbow grease

Part 6   Focus on Spoken Language

A) 2) 'one' refers to *coffee shop*
3) '*it*' refers to *coffee shop*; 'one' also refers to *coffee shop.*
4) '*It*" refers to *coffee shop*

B) Giving Advice

If I were you, *I'd write a list of the pros and cons of starting a business from scratch* or buying one that's already established and weigh up the possibilities on both sides before making any decisions.

C) Talking about Future Possibilities:

It'd save me a lot of time, money and hard work.

D) 'a lot of' and' 'a bit of' used with uncountable nouns

Don: ...But buying one that's already up and running would make it easier. It'd save a lot of *time, money and hard work*.

Don: Yes, I know it's a bit run-down but *a bit of elbow grease* will fix that

Don: Don't worry. I know there's *a lot to take into account*.

Don: ...I'll look into it *a lot more* before I make a final decision.

ANSWERS TO UNIT SIX - TALKING ABOUT THE PAST

Part 1

playful but unacceptable conduct - **_mischief_**	unhappy/angry because of problems - **_bitter_**
a sudden, bad experience - **_a shock_**	improve/return to a good situation - **_recover_**
being able to support yourself - **_independent_**	things that happen to us during life - **_experiences_**

1) a) party all weekend.

2) a) his parents had been killed in an accident.

3) a) he had learnt a lot from his experiences.

Part 5   Crossword

Across:
1. burn * the * candle * at * both * ends
3. keep * it * up
5. in * one * piece
7. stand * on * my * own * feet
9. around * the * corner

Down:
2. spur of the moment
4. takes * me * back
6. make * the * most * of
8. get * on * with
10. get * over
12. put * it * behind

Part 6   Focus on Spoken English

A)   1)   We used to get into some mischief.
We used to burn the candle at both ends most weekends.

2)   We'd party all night and then go straight to work the next day without any sleep.....or we'd drive across the country for the weekend on the spur of the moment.

3)   No, Dan doesn't do those things now.

C) Pronunciation - Words ending in 'ed'
Practice 1

Eve: Why, what happened /d/ to change things? /d/
Dan: Well, I was at work one day when I received /d/ the news that my parents had been killed /d/ in a car accident.
Eve: Oh no, that's terrible. I'm so sorry. You haven't talked /t/ about that before. It must have been a terrible shock.

Practice 2

ed pronounced as /d/	ed pronounced as /t/	ed pronounced as /əd/
loved	looked washed	waited started
arrived	worked	included

D) Pronouns in spoken English
1) 'that' refers to the crazy thing Dan used to do such as party all night, etc.

2) 'It' refers to the news that Dan's parents had been killed in a car accident

3) 'this' refers to the difficult experience of his parents' accident

1) E	4) I	7) C
2) F	5) D	8) B
3) H	6) G	9) A

ANSWERS TO UNIT SEVEN - ASKING FOR DIRECTIONS

Part 1 go around/stay away from - **avoid**   smaller/less busy streets - **back streets**
bridge over a road/railway - **overpass**   a curve/change in direction in a road - **bend**

1) b)   Fairgrove
2) a)   he's been in busy traffic for an hour   c) there are more one-way streets than before
3) a)   the old road.   b) through the back streets
4) b)   the back streets

Part 5 - Crossword

```
                        2
            1 a * s t o n e ' s * t h r o w
    4           r
    a           i                                    6
    *        3 c l e a r * s a i l i n g
    s           k                               e
  5 h a i r y                                   t
    o         8     10     7 h o l d * u p s
    r         a     t                     a
    t      12 *     u                     *
    *    9 b u m p e r * t o * b u m p e r
    c       o i     n                     o
    u       t l     *                     v
    t       t e     o                     e
            l *     f                     *
            e u                           o
            n p                           n
 11 f i n g e r s * c r o s s e d
            c
            k
```

Part   6   A) Giving Instructions

IMPERATIVE	SITUATION
Mix the sugar and milk together.	instruction for a recipe
Sit down and be quiet.	instruction from parent to small child
Go up the stairs and then turn right.	direction
Be careful!	warning regarding danger
Leave the building now!	a strong order
Deal five cards to each player.	instruction for a game

Attendant: **Watch out** for the trucks on that road though…
Driver: **Tell** me about it!

B)   Attendant: <u>**Do you**</u> need some help?
Driver: <u>**Do you**</u> mean back there, near the park?
Attendant: **It is** not a problem.

C)   Driver: Yes I see...on the other side of the highway.
Driver: You mean back there, near the park?

Part 1 an aim for the future **_goal_**   determined to be successful **_ambitious_**
unpaid work **_voluntary (work)_**   skills learned from practice **_experience_**
a useful situation, chance **_opportunity_**

1) b) visit his family;
   c) look for a job
2) a) do some voluntary work

3) a) people have to plan if they want to succeed.

4) a) ambitious.

Part 5 **Crossword**

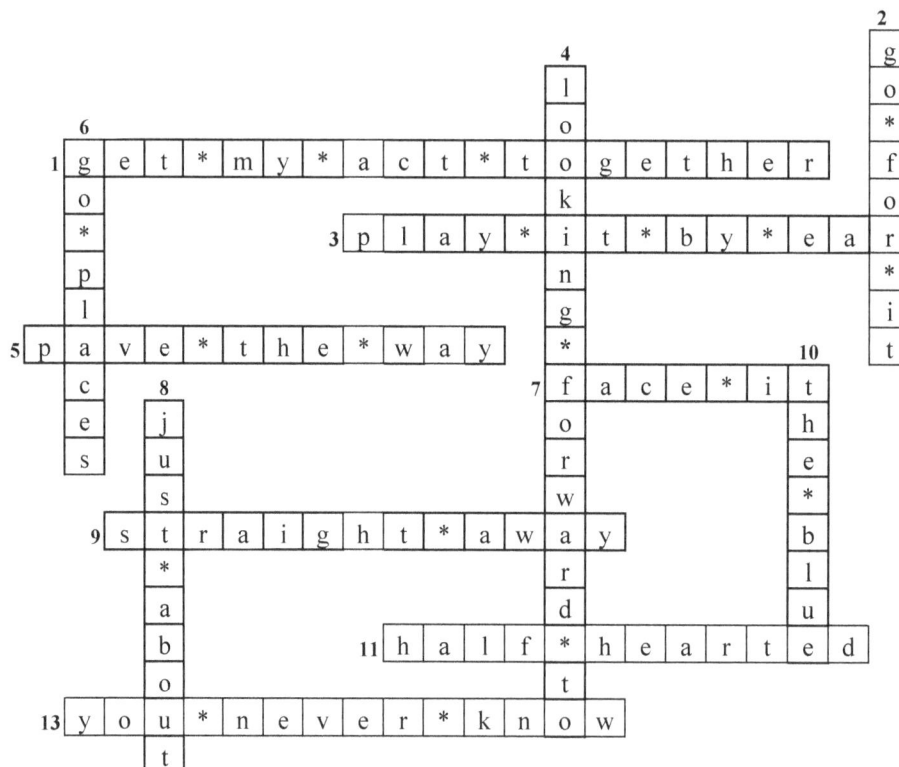

Across:
1. get * my * act * together
3. play * it * by * ear
5. pave * the * way
7. face * it
9. straight * away
11. half * hearted
13. you * never * know

Down:
2. go * for * it
4. looking * forward
6. go * places
8. just * about
10. the * blue

Part 6 **Focus on Spoken Language**

A) Talking about future plans and intentions

Exercise 1: Kerri: I suppose, I **_'ll_** just **_play_** it by ear.
Kerri: I guess, I **_'ll look_** for a job too…
Chris: I **_'ll_** just **_let_** the others know…

Exercise 2:
1st Speaker: This box is very heavy!   2nd Speaker: Wait a minute. I **_'ll help_** you.
1st Speaker: Oh, I forgot to post this letter! 2nd Speaker: Don't worry. I **_'ll post_** it later.

B) Talking about pre-planned decisions

Yes, I**'m**	**going to**	**visit** my family in the country for a week.
…… I**'m**	**going to**	**look** for a job…….as a tour guide if possible.
That's what I**'m**	**going to**	**do** if I don't get a job straight away.
Look, I**'m**	**going to**	**get** some lunch. How about you?

Practice

Sue: 'What are you going to do on Saturday?'
Pat: 'I'm not sure yet. I think I **_will_** stay home and study.'
Sue: 'Jenni and I are **_going to_** go to the beach. Would you like to come?'
Pat: 'Yes. That sounds great! I **_will_** finish my homework on Sunday instead.'
Sue: 'OK. We're **_going to_** catch the bus at 8 a.m.'
Pat: 'OK I **_will_** meet you at the bus stop then. What are you **_going to_** take for lunch?'
Sue: 'I'm not sure yet. I guess I **_will_** just take some fruit and a sandwich.'

C) Making Predictions

Kerri   ......I can see **_you're going to_** go places.

D) Talking about definite future arrangements

Chris: 'Yes, I'm going to visit my family in the country for a week. I'**_m flying_** out next Wednesday.'

Revision and Practice - Talking about the Future

Rai: What **_are_** you **_going to do_** while you're on holidays next week?

Jan: I **_am going to stay_** (or **_am staying_**) with my sister, Kate, and help her look after her two small sons.

Rai: Why? Is she sick?

Jan: No. She **_is going to have_** another baby. (or '**_is having_** another baby' - meaning at a future time)

Rai: Really? In that case, I **_will call_** her on the phone tonight and congratulate her.

Jan: Oh good! I'm sure, she **_will be_** happy to hear from you.

Rai: In fact, I think I **_will go_** to the shops tomorrow and buy a present for her. Any ideas?

Jan: Well, the weather **_is going to be_** (or **_will be_**) hot when the baby's born…

Rai: I know! I **_will buy_** her a fan!

Part 1

1) a) roast beef; b) vegetable loaf d) fish with chilli sauce

2) b) one

3) a) a comedy

Part 5   Crossword

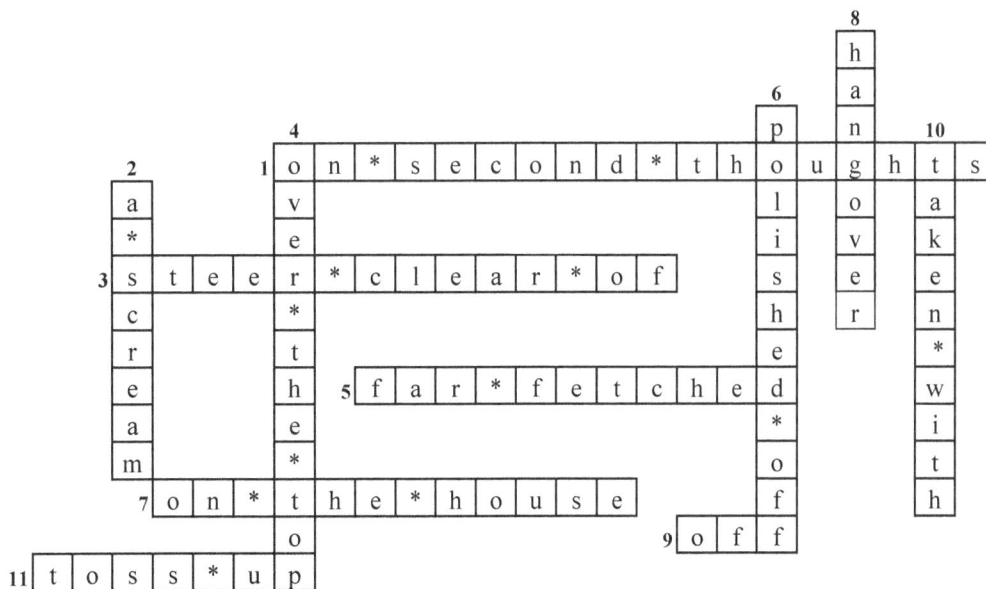

Across:
- 1 — on second thoughts
- 3 — steer clear of
- 5 — far fetched
- 7 — on the house
- 9 — off
- 11 — toss up

Down:
- 2 — a scream
- 4 — over the top
- 6 — polished off
- 8 — hangover
- 10 — taken with

Part 6   Focus on Spoken Language

A) 1) Me neither

Lee: Mm…I love seafood too but spicy food doesn't agree with me. So I **_won't_** have that.

Julie: **_Me neither_**. I'm going to steer clear of fish from now on. I had some that was off a few months ago and I can't stand it now.

2) Me too

> Lee: Now what'll I have…..I think, I'*ll* go for the vegetable loaf.
> Julie: *Me too*. The vegetarian food's always good here.

3) Practice

Bev: I *don't* eat dairy products these days. They don't agree with me.
Noni: Me *neither*. I'm allergic to milk.
Bev: I *can't* stand cheese.
Noni: Me *neither*. It makes me feel sick.
Bev: And I *don't* like yogurt.
Noni: Oh, I do. I think it's really nice. I have it occasionally with fruit and nuts.
Bev: But I love ice cream, of course, even though it's a dairy product.
Noni: Me *too*. It's delicious!

ANSWERS TO LANGUAGE REVIEW THREE

1) G		4) C		7) H	
2) D		5) E		8) B	
3) A		6) F		9) I	

EVERYDAY EXPRESSIONS	DEFINITIONS
hold the line…………………….…	wait a moment
put (you) through………………..…	connect you to the department/person
under way……………………….…	in progress
put (you) down ……………….……	write your name on the list
a rule of thumb………………….…	a rule for general guidance
cut off (date)………………….……	last possible (date)
take (your) details…………….……	record your name, address etc
the off chance……………….….…	the very small chance/slight possibility
pull out……………………….……	cancel/withdraw
red tape……………………….……	official rules and procedures
up in the air…………………….…..	undecided or uncertain
I wouldn't count on it………………..	don't expect it to happen/don't rely on it
ASAP - also a.s.a.p……………..………	as soon as possible
snapped up…………………….……	taken/accepted quickly
miss the boat………………….……	miss/lose an opportunity
(didn't) catch……………….………	(didn't) hear or understand

*Where a word appears between brackets (   ) in reference lists, it means that other pronouns or nouns may also be used in the expression.

EVERYDAY EXPRESSIONS	DEFINITIONS
What's up?............................	What's the problem?
not keeping up...........................	not progressing at the expected rate
too laid-back............................	too relaxed/lazy
a piece of cake..........................	an easy task
turn up to................................	arrive/attend
not up to par.............................	not of an acceptable standard/level
drop out	quit/stop participating
not cut out for............................	not suited to (something)
throw in the towel.......................	stop trying or stop participating
put in	(time/work) invest or invested
Come on!.................................	That's not true!
giving up.................................	quitting/stop trying
don't stand a chance.....................	have little or no chance of (success)
see (something) through.................	persist/continue (to completion)
knuckle down.............................	work hard
some pointers............................	some advice
get stuck into (it).......................	try hard/work hard
catch up..................................	reach/achieve the required level (after being behind)
get through...............................	pass/complete (a course)
give it a go...............................	try to do it
That's more like it!	That's a better idea!

EVERYDAY EXPRESSIONS	DEFINITIONS
looked over (something)	examined
go over (something)....................	review/discuss
enlarge on (something).................	explain in more detail
take for granted..........................	assume/suppose (something) will be known
spell out...................................	explain clearly
stand out...................................	be noticeable
sell yourself...............................	promote your value
something along the same lines.......	something similar to
keep going................................	continue
it just so happens........................	by chance
take it......................................	suppose/assume
come in handy...........................	be useful
a plus......................................	an advantage
fit the bill.................................	be exactly the right person (or thing) for the job
bring up to date….......................	change to include the most recent information
put together..............................	compose/produce
(be) looking at...........................	expect (a certain amount of money or time)
and so on..................................	and other things
look into it................................	investigate
(to) set up.................................	arrange/organise
brush up on...............................	revise/review/have practice
rusty..	weak/impaired due to lack of practice

EVERYDAY EXPRESSIONS

DEFINITIONS

EVERYDAY EXPRESSIONS	DEFINITIONS
falling off……………………………	decreasing
between you and me …………..………	this information is private (so don't tell anyone)
pointing the finger…………………..	saying the problem was caused by (someone)
go in for……………………..………	get/seek/show interest in (something)
hold our own……………………..………	keep/defend our position
go along with………………………..	agree with
bite the bullet...……………….….…	make an important/difficult decision
(being) up against………………….	competing with
folding…......………………………	failing/closing (relating to business)
jump on the bandwagon....…………	follow the popular course
go under………………………….....…	fail (in business)
be at the cutting edge……....……..	be involved with the latest developments
putting off.........……………........…	delaying/postponing
the bottom line……………….....…..	the basic truth
the sooner the better……….....………	as soon as possible
a vicious circle………………………	a cycle (of problems) in which the solution to one problem makes more problems
mind-boggling...............................…	amazing/ unbelievable/difficult to understand
get my head around…………………	understand/accept (something new)
go with the flow……………………	accept and progress with changes (in life)
get the ball rolling………………......……	start the project or activity

EVERYDAY EXPRESSIONS

toying with the idea…………………	
came across……................…………	
going for a song……………………..	
take the plunge………...........………..	
from scratch………………………....	
up and running………………………	
through the grapevine…………........	
going downhill………………………	
get rid of…………...........……………	
run-down……………………………	
elbow grease…………………………	
(an idea) up my sleeve………………	
get (something) off the ground………	
talk (you) out of it……………………	
get your fingers burned.……………..	
pros and cons…………………………	
weigh up ……………………………..	
take into account……………………..	
look into (it).………………………..	
drawbacks..	
do (my) homework……..........……...	
go ahead………………………………	

DEFINITIONS

thinking about

found by chance

being sold very cheaply

take the important step

from the beginning without help

operating

information heard from other people

not doing well/deteriorating

dispose of (something)

neglected/ in a bad condition

hard work/physical effort

(an idea) in my mind (to use later)

get (something) into successful operation

tell (you) not to do something/discourage (you)

have a bad experience (often related to money)

advantages and disadvantages

consider

think about

investigate

disadvantages

research/investigate/check

continue/proceed

EVERYDAY EXPRESSIONS

takes me back………………………..

to get into (some mischief)...............

It's a wonder………………………..

in one piece…………………………

crazy…………………………………

burn the candle at both ends………..

on the spur of the moment…………

keep (that) up………………………

turned upside down ………………..

get over (it)…………………………

I'd rather not go into it......…………

strike me as (something)…......……

put this behind me......………....…

get on with (something)……………

haven't looked back…………………

turned out (differently)……………..

stand on my own feet………………

around the corner……………………

make the most of ……………..………

DEFINITIONS

makes me remember

involved in (playful, but unacceptable activity)

I'm surprised

alive and unharmed

foolish (but exciting)

have little sleep (due to too much activity)

suddenly, without planning

continue with (that activity)

completely changed (in a negative way)

recover from (the experience)

I'd rather not talk about/discuss it.

seem/appear to me as (something)

recover from (this unhappy experience)

proceed/continue with (something)

have progressed/succeeded

had a different result

be independent

in the future

fully use and enjoy

EVERYDAY EXPRESSIONS

after ....

a bottleneck......................................

Tell me about it!......................

bumper to bumper traffic..................

backed up (traffic).......................

a pile up.................................

(something) has thrown me............

turn off.................................

tricky.......................................

Watch out for...........................

hairy.......................................

I'll keep that in mind..................

a short cut......................................

a stone's throw.................................

clear sailing.............................

your safest bet..........................

get a move on..........................

keep my fingers crossed..............

hold ups...

DEFINITIONS

seeking/looking for

a crowded section of road

I agree!/I know!

very slow moving traffic

in a queue of congested traffic

a road accident involving several vehicles

(something) has made me confused

turn into a side road (when driving)

difficult/confusing

be careful of (something)

frightening/dangerous

I'll remember that.

a shorter/quicker way

a short distance

easy to do/achieve

the best choice

hurry

wish for luck and success

delays

EVERYDAY EXPRESSIONS	DEFINITIONS
just about……………………………	almost
play it by ear………………………..	wait and see what happens (not have plans)
looking forward to…………………	happily awaiting (something)
half hearted (about)…………………	disinterested (only half interested)
let's face it...	we must accept the truth about this situation
every Tom, Dick and Harry…………	a lot of (ordinary) people
straight away………………………..	immediately
twiddling my thumbs………………	doing nothing; being bored
taken with the idea…………………	happy about the idea
killing two birds with one stone…….	achieving two things/results with one action
paving the way………………………	preparing the way
you never know……………………..	there is a possibility
have to hand it to (you)……………..	have to admire/congratulate (you)
have it all worked out………………	have everything planned and organised
turn up………………………………	arrive/occur/happen
out of the blue..............................……..	unexpectedly (without planning)
as far as I'm concerned……………	in my opinion
set (our) sights on…………………..	decide and aim for (something)
go for it!……………………………	strive/try hard (to get what we want)
go places..	be successful
get my act together…………………	get organised

EVERYDAY EXPRESSIONS

a toss up.................................

doesn't agree with me...................

steer clear of...........................

off.......................................

can't stand..............................

on the house.............................

I don't blame you........................

go for...................................

(the drinks) are on me...................

round (of drinks)........................

I'm easy.................................

on second thoughts.......................

a hangover...............................

polish off...............................

a scream.................................

in stitches..............................

taken with...............................

over the top ....

far-fetched..............................

check it out.............................

DEFINITIONS

a choice/decision between two options

isn't good for my health

avoid

bad/stale (food)

dislike very much

at no cost (at the management's expense)

I understand your decision.

choose/have

my expense/I will pay for you.

a set of drinks (one for each person)

I'll be happy with either choice/I don't mind.

after thinking more about (it)

a headache etc. caused by too much alcohol

finish completely

a very funny (thing)

laughing very much

impressed with (something)

exaggerated/extreme

unbelievable - difficult to believe it is possible

see/investigate it

Reference page
Some notable pronunciation differences between varieties of English

Words containing the letter 'a'

Many English words, containing the letter 'a' (eg. answer) may be pronounced as a short sound /æ/ or a long sound /ɑ:/ depending on which variety of English is being spoken. See the table below which shows examples of pronunciation differences across varieties of English.

Spelling	Examples of pronunciation differences for the following words.		
ask passed last laugh can't half plant	/æsk/ /pæst/ /læst/ /læf/ /kænt/ /hæf/ /plænt/	may be pronounced as the vowel sound /æ/ as in *black hat*.	/ɑ:sk/ /pɑ:st/ /lɑ:st/ /lɑ:f/ /kɑ:nt/ /hɑ:f/ /plɑ:nt/ may be pronounced as the lengthened vowel sound /ɑ:/ as in *large heart*.

Words containing the letter 'o'

There are differences between North American English and British English in the pronunciation of some words containing the letter 'o'. For example, in British English, the words *stop*, *dot*, *lock* are pronounced with the vowel sound /ɒ/. These words, in North American English, are pronounced with the vowel sound /ɑ/, a slightly longer sound. For example, in North American English the words *lock* and *lark* are pronounced with the same vowel sound /ɑ/, whereas in British English *lock* is pronounced /lɒk/ and *lark* is pronounced /lɑ:k/.

Words containing the letter 'r'

In all varieties of English, the letter 'r' in written words, is pronounced clearly in speech when followed by a vowel sound. For example, 'r' is generally pronounced clearly where it is followed by a vowel sound in the same word, eg. right, roll, paragraph; or when 'r' is followed by a vowel sound in the following word, eg. wear it; door open; for example.

However, where the letter 'r' is followed by a consonant sound or when it occurs at the end of an utterance, speakers of some varieties of English (Australian/South African/Southern British and other varieties) omit the sound /r/. Speakers of North American English (and other varieties), on the other hand, always pronounce 'r', regardless of its position in a word or utterance.

Spelling	Examples of pronunciation differences for words containing the letter 'r'		
car sport sister four	/kɑ:r/ /spɔ:rt/ /sɪstər/ /fɔ:r/	Generally, speakers of North American, Canadian, Scottish, Irish (and others) pronounce the letter 'r' regardless of its position in a word.	/kɑ:/ /spɔ:t/ /sɪstə/ /fɔ:/ Generally, speakers of Australian, Southern British, South African, and New Zealand English do **not** pronounce 'r' when it is followed by a consonant sound.

Phonemic Chart of English Sounds

Below each sound symbol are examples of words containing the sound.

Vowel sounds

æ (short sound) bl**a**ck	**e** (short sound) r**e**d	**ɒ** (British English only) …. d**o**ts ….	**ə** (unstressed sound) oth**er** broth**er**
ɑ: (long sound) *st**ars**	**ʊ** (short sound) g**oo**d	**ʌ** (short sound) f**u**n	**ɪ** (short sound) p**i**nk
ɜ: (long sound) *p**ur**ple	**u:** (long sound) bl**ue**	**ɔ:** (long sound) *f**our** m**ore**	**i:** (long sound) gr**ee**n

As the pronunciation of some English vowel sounds varies across and within countries, the example words are intended as a *general* guide.

Diphthong (two vowel) sounds

eɪ gr**ey**	**ɔɪ** b**oy**	**əʊ** (also oʊ) yell**ow** g**o**ld	**ɪə** cl**ear** b**eer**
eə (also ɛə) h**air**	**aɪ** br**i**ght l**i**me	**ʊə** t**our** (also /tʊr/	**aʊ** br**ow**n m**ou**se

Consonant sounds

p **p**et **p**ig	**b** **b**ig **b**ag	**t** **t**ell **t**wo	**d** **d**irty **d**og
tʃ **Ch**inese **ch**ild	**dʒ** **j**ust **j**oking	**k** **k**eep **c**ool	**g** **g**ood **g**irl
f **f**ill **f**our	**v** **v**ery **v**ivid	**θ** **th**ink **th**in	**ð** o**th**er bro**th**er
s **s**ad **s**ong	**z** **z**ig-**z**ag	**ʃ** **sh**ort **sh**eep	**ʒ** mea**s**ure A**s**ia
m **m**ilk **m**an	**n** **n**o **n**ever	**ŋ** lo**ng** so**ng**	**h** **h**ot **h**ill
l **l**ittle **l**ine	**r** **r**ice	**w** **w**et **w**inter	**j** **y**es **y**ou

*Note: In some varieties of English, the letter 'r' is clearly pronounced wherever it occurs in words, (eg. star, purple, four), however in some varieties of English, 'r' is only pronounced when it is followed by a vowel sound.

© Boyer Educational Resources, 2003

Boyer Educational Resources books and audio CDs

www.boyereducation.com.au   www.englishebooks.com

NEW in 2014
Rhyming Stories

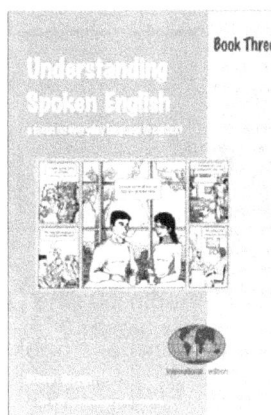

'**Understanding Spoken English**' – (books with audio CDs)

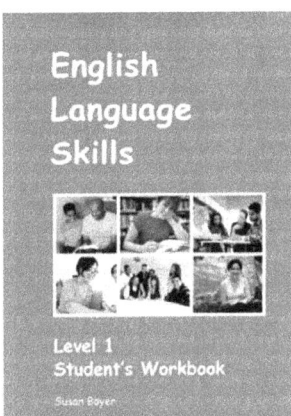

includes storybook,
language workbook
and audio CD

English Language Skills
Level One

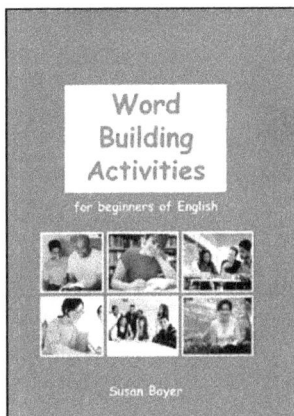

Word Building Activities
for beginners of English

Understanding English
Pronunciation

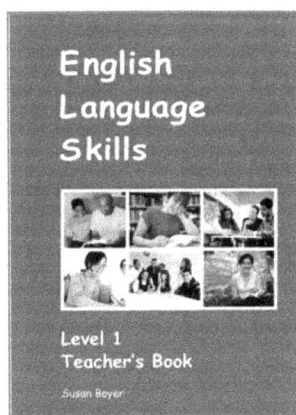

English Language Skills
Teacher's Book

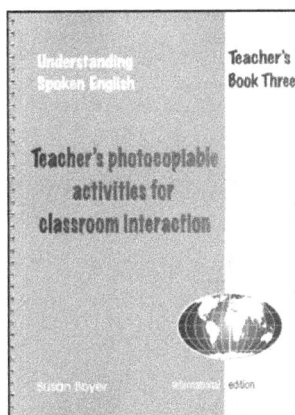

Understanding Spoken English
Teacher's Book

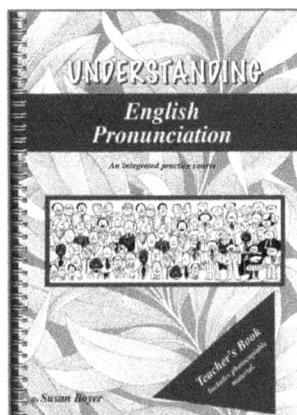

Understanding English
Pronunciation
Teacher's Book

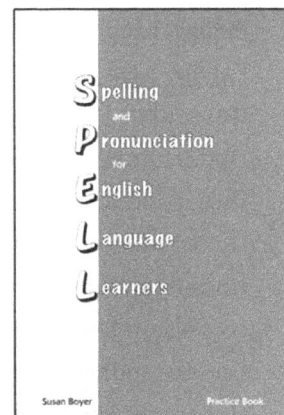

Spelling and Pronunciation
for English Language Learners

Spiral bound Teacher's Books contain photocopiable activity pages, such as surveys,
role cards & matching activities. All our teacher's books are A4 size.
Student books contain language exercises and answers.

www.boyereducation.com for details of all publications by Boyer Educational Resources

www.englishebooks.com for details of e-book versions of these resources

Boyer Educational Resources

Office phone/fax: +61 (0)2 4739 1538   e-mail: boyer@eftel.net.au
websites: www.boyereducation.com.au   www.englishebooks.com

Title	ISBN
Rhyming Stories - practice with the sounds and spelling of English (A5)	978 1 877074 06 6
Rhyming Stories -audio CD	978 1 877074 37 0
Rhyming Stories - language workbook (A4)	978 1 877074 38 7
Understanding Spoken English - Book One	978 1 877074 08 0
Understanding Spoken English - Audio CD One (1)	978 1 877074 10 3
Understanding Spoken English - Teacher's Book One	978 1 877074 11 0
Understanding Spoken English – Book One & Audio CD	**978 1 877074 18 9**
Understanding Spoken English - Book Two	978 1 877074 12 7
Understanding Spoken English - Audio CD Two (1)	978 1 877074 14 1
Understanding Spoken English - Teacher's Book Two	978 1 877074 15 8
Understanding Spoken English – Book Two & Audio CD	**978 1 877074 19 6**
Understanding Spoken English - Book Three	978 1 877074 24 0
Understanding Spoken English - Audio CD Three	978 1 877074 25 7
Understanding Spoken English - Teacher's Book Three	978 1 877074 26 4
Understanding Spoken English – Book Three & Audio CD	**978 1 877074 27 1**
Spelling and Pronunciation for English Language Learners	978 1 877074 04 2
Understanding English Pronunciation - Student book only	978 0 9585395 7 9
Understanding English Pronunciation - Audio CD (Set of 3)	978 1 877074 03 5
Understanding English Pronunciation - Teacher's Book	978 0 9585395 9 3
Word Building Activities for Beginners of English	978 1 877074 28 8
English Language Skills – Level One Student's Workbook	978 1 877074 29 5
English Language Skills – Level One Audio CD	978 1 877074 31 8
English Language Skills – Level One Teacher's Book	978 1 877074 32 5
Resources with an Australian focus:	
Understanding Everyday Australian - Book One	978 0 9585395 0 0
Understanding Everyday Australian - Audio CD One (1)	978 1 877074 01 1
Understanding Everyday Australian - Teacher's Book One	978 0 9585395 2 4
Understanding Everyday Australian - Book One & Audio CD	**978 1 877074 16 5**
Understanding Everyday Australian - Book Two	978 0 9585395 3 1
Understanding Everyday Australian - Audio CD Two (1)	978 1 877074 02 8
Understanding Everyday Australian - Teacher's Book Two	978 0 9585395 5 5
Understanding Everyday Australian - Book Two & Audio CD Pack	**978 1 877074 17 2**
Understanding Everyday Australian - Book Three	978 1 877074 20 2
Understanding Everyday Australian - Audio CD Three	978 1 877074 21 9
Understanding Everyday Australian - Teacher's Book Three	978 1 877074 22 6
Understanding Everyday Australian - Book Three & Audio CD	**978 1 877074 23 3**
People in Australia's past - their stories, their achievements - A5 Reader	978 1 877074 34 9
People in Australia's past - audio CD	978 1 877074 35 6
People in Australia's past - language workbook A4 (156 pages)	978 1 877074 36 3

Visit our website **www.boyereducation.com.au** for a distributor near you.

www.ingramcontent.com/pod-product-compliance
Lightning Source LLC
Chambersburg PA
CBHW081136090426
42742CB00015BA/2865